Learning Azure DocumentDB

Create outstanding enterprise solutions around
DocumentDB using the latest technologies and
programming tools with Azure

Riccardo Becker

[PACKT] enterprise
PUBLISHING professional expertise distilled

BIRMINGHAM - MUMBAI

Learning Azure DocumentDB

First published: November 2015

Production reference: 1161115

Published by Packt Publishing Ltd.
Livery Place
35 Livery Street
Birmingham B3 2PB, UK.

ISBN 978-1-78355-246-7

www.packtpub.com

Credits

Author
Riccardo Becker

Reviewers
Rémon ter Haar
Juan Carlos Sánchez

Commissioning Editor
Neil Alexander

Acquisition Editor
Kirk D'costa

Content Development Editor
Samantha Gonsalves

Technical Editor
Madhunikita Sunil Chindarkar

Copy Editor
Roshni Banerjee

Project Coordinator
Sanchita Mandal

Proofreader
Safis Editing

Indexer
Priya Sane

Production Coordinator
Nitesh Thakur

Cover Work
Nitesh Thakur

About the Author

Riccardo Becker works full time as a principal IT architect for CGI in the Netherlands. He holds several certifications and his background in computing goes way back to 1998, when he started working with good old Visual Basic 5.0 (or was it 6.0?). Ever since, he has fulfilled several roles, such as a developer, lead developer, architect, project leader, practice manager. Recently, he decided to accept the role of a principal IT architect where he focuses on innovation, cutting-edge technology, and specifically on Microsoft Azure, the Internet of Things, and cloud computing in general.

In 2007, he joined the Microsoft LEAP program where he got a peek at the move Microsoft was about to make on their road to the cloud. Pat Helland gave him that insight, and since the first release of Microsoft Azure on PDC 2008, he started to focus on it, keeping track of the progress and the maturity of the platform. In the past few years, he has also done a lot of work on incubation with his employer, raising awareness of cloud computing in general and Microsoft Azure in particular.

I would like to thank all my colleagues who have helped me on various subjects inside the world of Azure. Special thanks go to Rémon ter Haar and Juan Carlos Sánchez who were patient enough to review my chapters. Thanks Rémon and Juan!

I would also like to thank the folks from Packt Publishing who helped me stay on track and on schedule despite some bummers and some changes that I made to the original outline.

Special thanks to my employer CGI for giving me all the opportunities and interesting projects that have helped me in realizing this book. Thanks to my daily job and the ability to focus on the subjects, I have come to the point of having enough knowledge to write this book.

This is my second published book, since I have already published *Windows Azure Programming Patterns for Start-ups*, also with the help of Packt Publishing.

About the Reviewers

Rémon ter Haar is highly experienced in designing and implementing Microsoft technology-based solutions. He has worked as a technical solution architect and lead developer in various projects. For the last 8 years, he has been specializing as a system integrator using Microsoft BizTalk technology and Microsoft Azure. He currently works at Motion10 (www.motion10.nl) as a BizTalk consultant. Motion10 is the leading competence center in the Netherlands when it comes to system integration, SharePoint, Office 365, BI, and Internet of Things.

He has also reviewed *Windows Azure Programming Patterns for Start-ups*.

Juan Carlos Sánchez is a software engineer and he writes code for fun. He loves to work in teams and is familiar with the SCRUM process and Agile Release Train.

He has experience of the following applications:

- Desktop windows applications (WPF)
- Cross-platform phone applications (Cordova and Ionic)
- Azure: Cloud services, Active Directory, and web applications (AngularJS)
- Databases: Entity Framework SQL Server, DocumentDB, and Azure Storage
- He contributes to the community with his blog and code at the following links:
    - http://www.softwarejuancarlos.com
    - http://github.com/softwarejc

To my family and girlfriend—I love you.

www.PacktPub.com

Support files, eBooks, discount offers, and more

For support files and downloads related to your book, please visit www.PacktPub.com.

Did you know that Packt offers eBook versions of every book published, with PDF and ePub files available? You can upgrade to the eBook version at www.PacktPub.com and as a print book customer, you are entitled to a discount on the eBook copy. Get in touch with us at service@packtpub.com for more details.

At www.PacktPub.com, you can also read a collection of free technical articles, sign up for a range of free newsletters and receive exclusive discounts and offers on Packt books and eBooks.

PACKTLiB™

https://www2.packtpub.com/books/subscription/packtlib

Do you need instant solutions to your IT questions? PacktLib is Packt's online digital book library. Here, you can search, access, and read Packt's entire library of books.

Why subscribe?

- Fully searchable across every book published by Packt
- Copy and paste, print, and bookmark content
- On demand and accessible via a web browser

Free access for Packt account holders

If you have an account with Packt at www.PacktPub.com, you can use this to access PacktLib today and view 9 entirely free books. Simply use your login credentials for immediate access.

Instant updates on new Packt books

Get notified! Find out when new books are published by following @PacktEnterprise on Twitter or the *Packt Enterprise* Facebook page.

Table of Contents

Preface

In August 2014, Microsoft announced the preview of their DocumentDB service offering. DocumentDB is a NoSQL database that meets the requirements of today's applications that evolve at a higher pace, including modifications to the data model. DocumentDB covers all this by offering a schema-free document database that offers flexibility, scalability, automated indexing, and a mature range of querying possibilities. Recently, Microsoft announced support for geospatial indexing and querying, opening a whole new range of possibilities.

Setting an example, Microsoft utilizes DocumentDB in its renewed `http://www.msn.com`, servicing 450 million unique monthly visitors. 25 percent of these visitors have their own personalized data and this data is services from DocumentDB.

DocumentDB greatly enhances the flexibility of your evolving applications and offers a rich querying environment for any kind of data that you store.

This book covers all the concepts and possibilities of DocumentDB by covering the theory with lots of examples in every chapter. This book is linear and every chapter builds on the knowledge of the last. For the more experienced users, chapters can also be read individually and in any order.

By the end of this book, you will be able to use DocumentDB in your own daily work and benefit from best practices.

What this book covers

Chapter 1, Getting Started with DocumentDB, covers the basics of DocumentDB. It explores the data model and compares DocumentDB with other NoSQL technologies. It also outlines the pricing model of DocumentDB. By the end of this chapter, we will learn how to set up a DocumentDB environment and how to prepare Visual Studio 2015 to start building solutions using DocumentDB.

Chapter 2, Setting up and Managing Your Database, provides detailed information on how to set up, maintain, and manage your DocumentDB. It also covers how to monitor your DocumentDB and, based on monitoring results, reconfigure DocumentDB.

Chapter 3, Basic Querying, provides an insight into the basic querying options for DocumentDB. It covers how to create, update, read, and delete documents from your DocumentDB in the most basic form.

Chapter 4, Advanced Querying, provides an insight into all the possibilities in the SQL grammar that is available for DocumentDB.

Chapter 5, Using REST to Access Your Database, discusses how to use DocumentDB using the open REST protocol. It also covers how to use JavaScript to work with DocumentDB and how to authenticate and execute queries.

Chapter 6, Using Node.js to Access Your Database, provides a detailed description of how to use DocumentDB features with Node.js

Chapter 7, Advanced Techniques, covers indexes and how to use them effectively. It also covers how to measure the performance of our database and use partitioning techniques.

Chapter 8, Putting Your Database at the Heart of Azure Solutions, describes patterns that can be applied to your Azure solution, collaborating with DocumentDB. It also covers some patterns and how to integrate DocumentDB inside your current Azure solution by replacing some of the current data repositories, which will be moved to DocumentDB.

What you need for this book

The softwares that are needed to follow the examples outlined in this book are as follows:

- Visual Studio 2015 (any version)
- Azure SDK 2.7
- DocumentDB .NET SDK Version 1.5
- An Azure subscription
- A modern browser

Who this book is for

This book is for novice developers and database architects who need a thorough knowledge of the features of DocumentDB to develop applications with it. Basic knowledge of SQL would be helpful.

Conventions

In this book, you will find a number of text styles that distinguish between different kinds of information. Here are some examples of these styles and an explanation of their meaning.

Code words in text, database table names, folder names, filenames, file extensions, pathnames, dummy URLs, user input, and Twitter handles are shown as follows: "A good example of a UDF is a function called `calculateAge()` that takes the date of birth of a person and returns the age as a value."

A block of code is set as follows:

```
User user = await client.ReadUserAsync(readUser.SelfLink);

FeedResponse<Permission> permissions = await
  client.ReadPermissionFeedAsync(readUser.SelfLink);
foreach (var permission in permissions)
{
  Console.WriteLine(permission.Id + ":" +
    permission.ResourceLink + ":" +
    permission.PermissionMode.ToString());
}
```

New terms and **important words** are shown in bold. Words that you see on the screen, for example, in menus or dialog boxes, appear in the text like this: "Click on the **New Support** button and follow the wizard that shows up."

> Warnings or important notes appear in a box like this.

> Tips and tricks appear like this.

Reader feedback

Feedback from our readers is always welcome. Let us know what you think about this book—what you liked or disliked. Reader feedback is important for us as it helps us develop titles that you will really get the most out of.

To send us general feedback, simply e-mail feedback@packtpub.com, and mention the book's title in the subject of your message.

If there is a topic that you have expertise in and you are interested in either writing or contributing to a book, see our author guide at www.packtpub.com/authors.

Customer support

Now that you are the proud owner of a Packt book, we have a number of things to help you to get the most from your purchase.

Downloading the example code

You can download the example code files from your account at http://www.packtpub.com for all the Packt Publishing books you have purchased. If you purchased this book elsewhere, you can visit http://www.packtpub.com/support and register to have the files e-mailed directly to you.

Downloading the color images of this book

We also provide you with a PDF file that has color images of the screenshots/ diagrams used in this book. The color images will help you better understand the changes in the output. You can download this file from http://www.packtpub.com/sites/default/files/downloads/2467EN_ColorImages.pdf.

Errata

Although we have taken every care to ensure the accuracy of our content, mistakes do happen. If you find a mistake in one of our books—maybe a mistake in the text or the code—we would be grateful if you could report this to us. By doing so, you can save other readers from frustration and help us improve subsequent versions of this book. If you find any errata, please report them by visiting http://www.packtpub.com/submit-errata, selecting your book, clicking on the **Errata Submission Form** link, and entering the details of your errata. Once your errata are verified, your submission will be accepted and the errata will be uploaded to our website or added to any list of existing errata under the Errata section of that title.

To view the previously submitted errata, go to https://www.packtpub.com/books/content/support and enter the name of the book in the search field. The required information will appear under the **Errata** section.

Piracy

Piracy of copyrighted material on the Internet is an ongoing problem across all media. At Packt, we take the protection of our copyright and licenses very seriously. If you come across any illegal copies of our works in any form on the Internet, please provide us with the location address or website name immediately so that we can pursue a remedy.

Please contact us at copyright@packtpub.com with a link to the suspected pirated material.

We appreciate your help in protecting our authors and our ability to bring you valuable content.

Questions

If you have a problem with any aspect of this book, you can contact us at questions@packtpub.com, and we will do our best to address the problem.

1
Getting Started with DocumentDB

Until recently, the most common answer to the question "Where do I store my application information?" was *in a relational database, obviously*. The answer to this simple yet meaningful question is not so straightforward anymore.

NoSQL databases are becoming more and more popular and DocumentDB is one of them. In August 2014, Scott Guthrie officially announced the first preview version of DocumentDB. DocumentDB is a NoSQL database service offered by Microsoft. It is delivered as a managed service on Azure. This means that we no longer have to manage any infrastructure; we can just take it from the tap and pay per use. DocumentDB is a schema-free store, which means that we can store any kind of JSON document inside the store and work with the data as we used to in traditional SQL databases.

In this chapter, we will do the following:

- Learn what DocumentDB is all about
- Look at the data model
- Make a comparison with other non-SQL technologies
- Learn about the pricing model
- Build a console application that connects to a database

This book is aimed at architects, developers, database administrators, and IT professionals who want to learn and understand the breadth of DocumentDB.

What is DocumentDB?

The short answer to this question is that DocumentDB is a managed JSON document database service. But what is the impact on our programming paradigms? How can we use it? Why should we use it? Can it really make our life easier? The answers to these kinds of questions are a bit more involved and need additional clarification.

This section describes the fundamentals of DocumentDB and can help you decide whether or not it will be a good fit for your solution.

Microsoft built DocumentDB from the ground up because the feedback they got from customers was that they "...need a database that can keep pace with their rapidly evolving applications...." Schema-free databases are increasingly popular, but running these on our premises can be expensive and difficult to scale. Combining this with the need for rich querying and transactions still being available, Microsoft decided to build DocumentDB.

This brings us to the longer version of our answer, which is that DocumentDB is a "...a massively scalable, schema-free database with rich query and transaction processing using the most ubiquitous programming language, JavaScript, data model (JSON), and transport protocol (HTTP)..." (`http://blogs.msdn.com/b/documentdb/archive/2014/08/22/introducing-azure-documentdb-microsoft-s-fully-managed-nosql-document-database-service.aspx`).

The characteristics of a schema

As stated before, NoSQL databases are gaining popularity and are slowly replacing traditional relational databases. The main characteristics of a NoSQL database are listed next:

- Schema-less, with the ability to store *everything*
- Non-relational
- Extremely scalable

> Besides DocumentDB databases, there are other NoSQL databases available, such as graphs and key-value databases. We will study a comparison later in this chapter.

Having no schema (or predefined structure like tables and columns) allows us to store *everything*. This also includes attachments, user-defined functions, stored procedures, triggers, and more. The only restriction is that the information has to be in valid JSON.

Having JavaScript at the core

The SQL language that can be used to query and manipulate DocumentDB is based on JavaScript. Having JavaScript at the core means that we do not need to learn new techniques or languages, and our current knowledge of JavaScript can be applied immediately. Using JavaScript is a natural way of working with JSON. JSON parsers are perfectly capable of converting query results into variables, manipulating them, and writing them back to the database. Besides working as a *client* with JavaScript, the internals are also based on JavaScript. The following entities are written in JavaScript as well:

- **Stored procedures (SPs)**: These are executed by issuing an HTTP POST request. Inside the SP, the elements of the designated document(s) are copied to ordinary JavaScript variables. The logic inside the SP then manipulates the data and when the SP finishes, the values are persisted in the document(s) again.

- **User-defined functions (UDFs)**: The difference between UDFs and SP is that UDFs do not manipulate databases or documents themselves. A UDF encapsulates logic or business rules that can be called from SP or queries and can help extend the query language. A good example of a UDF is a function called `calculateAge()` that takes the date of birth of a person and returns their age as a value. The `calculateAge()` function can be used from a query returning only those persons that are older than 40 years. The query is as follows:

  ```
  SELECT * from people p where calculateAge(p.dob) > 40,
  ```

- **Triggers**: A trigger is a piece of JavaScript code (comparable to UDFs and SPs), but which is only invoked after some event that happens inside your database. A document being created or deleted could result in a trigger being executed. Triggers can be executed *before* or *after* the actual event happens. When a trigger fails or raises an exception, the actual operation is aborted and the transaction is not committed but rolled back. This is useful when we need to validate the incoming data to keep our documents consistent.

We will provide extensive examples of SPs, user-defined functions and triggers later in this book.

Indexing a document

In traditional relational databases, the DBA or developer needs to choose the (clustered) indexes. Choosing the right indexing strategy is vital for the performance and consistency of the database.

In DocumentDB, we do not need to choose the index ourselves. In fact, all information inside a document is indexed. This means that we can query on any attribute that is available inside the document. We can choose different *indexing policies*, but for most applications the default indexing policy will be the best choice between performance and storage efficiency. We can reduce storage space by excluding certain paths within the document used for indexing.

The indexing process inside DocumentDB treats the documents as trees. There needs to be a top node that is the entry point for all the fields inside the document. Imagine a document containing information about a person in the following JSON representation:

```
{
    "firstname": "John",
    "lastname": "Doe",
    "dob", "01-01-1960",
    "hobbies":
    [
        { "type":"sports", "description":"soccer"},
        { "type":"reading", "preferences":
          [
            { "type":"scifi"},
            { "type":"thriller"}
          ]
        }
    ]
}
```

This JSON snippet describes a person, John Doe, who was born on January 1, 1960, and has two hobbies, sports and reading. His reading hobby focuses on the sci-fi and thriller genres.

A JSON document can be depicted like this:

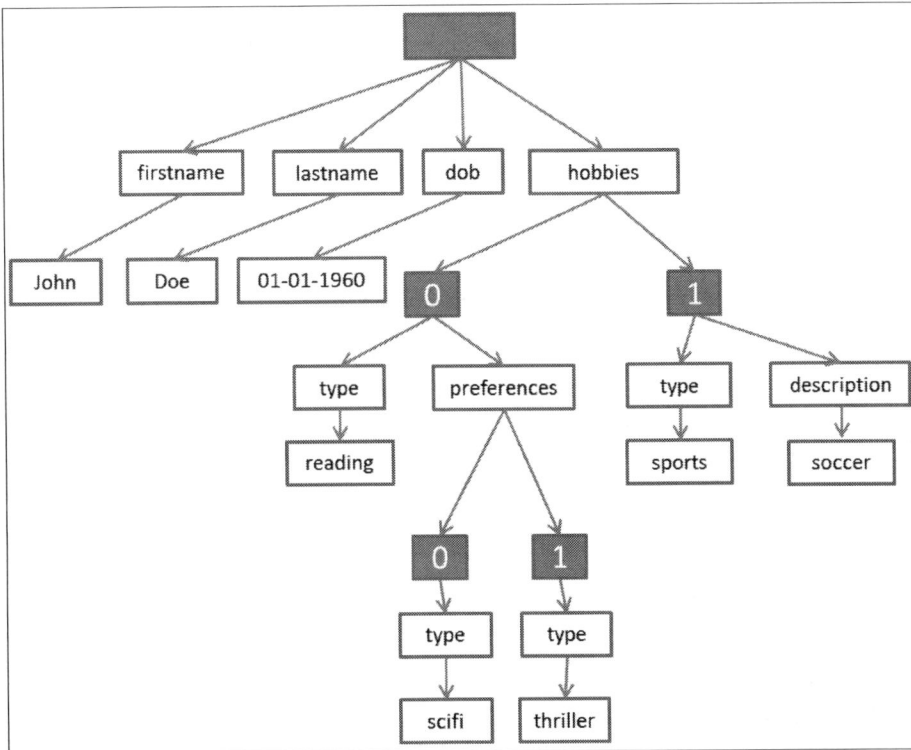

The blue squares are nodes that are implicitly added by the system and do not influence our data model. The figure shows that documents are internally represented as trees. As you can see, the nodes that describe a hobby do not necessary have to be the same in schema. Go ahead and try to build this model in a traditional relational database system!

DocumentDB as a service

Microsoft offers DocumentDB as part of their online offerings on the Microsoft Azure platform. Their *as-a-service* approach enables developers to start using new technologies immediately.

Understanding performance

The performance of our DocumentDB system is influenced by a *performance level*. Performance levels are set on a collection and not a database. This enables fine-tuning of your environment, giving the appropriate performance boost to the right resources. Setting the performance level influences the number of so-called request units. A request unit is a measure for the resources (CPU, memory) needed to perform a certain operation.

There are three performance levels:

- **S1**: Allows up to 250 request units per second
- **S2**: Allows up to 1,000 request units per second
- **S3**: Allows up to 2,500 request units per second

We need to choose the performance level carefully, since it comes with a price impact. We will discuss the pricing of DocumentDB later in this chapter.

Handling transactions

DocumentDB also supports transactions providing **Atomicity**, **Consistency**, **Isolation**, **Durability (ACID)** guarantees. Atomicity enables all operations to be executed as a single piece of work, all being committed at once or not at all. Consistency implies that all data is in the right state across transactions. Isolation makes sure that transactions do not interfere with each other, and durability ensures that all changes that are committed to the database will always be available.

Since JavaScript is executing under snapshot isolation belonging to the collection, SPs and triggers are executed within the same scope, enabling ACID for all operations inside SPs and triggers. If an error occurs in the JavaScript logic, the transaction is automatically rolled back.

Common use cases

Now that we have seen a little of DocumentDB, how can we decide whether DocumentDB is applicable for our own problem scenario? In which scenarios is it a good fit and are there any trade-offs?

Building the Internet of Things

A good example of a problem domain in which DocumentDB fits is the domain of the **Internet of Things (IoT)**. The IoT is all about ingesting, egressing, processing, and storing data (visit `https://en.wikipedia.org/wiki/Internet_of_Things`). It involves data flowing to and from devices, backend services processing that data or controlling devices, storage services persisting that data, or running statistical analysis or analytics on that data. Because DocumentDB can connect to HDInsight (`http://azure.microsoft.com/en-us/services/hdinsight/`) and Hadoop, the data can be analyzed easily.

Another good area in the IoT domain is device registration. Each and every device in the field is described inside a single document and stored in DocumentDB. These documents contain information for the device to be able to play the game of IoT, having keys and endpoints to communicate with and enable ingress and egress dataflows.

Throughout this book, we will also take the IoT domain as our main example domain. Examples and code snippets will focus on this area because it is a good area to project the possibilities of DocumentDB on.

Storing user profile information

Storing user profile information inside DocumentDB can be really helpful when it comes to personalized user interfaces or other preferences that can influence an application's behavior or user interface settings.

> JavaScript can easily interpret JSON data and is therefore an excellent candidate for describing the markup of a personalized user interface. Extending this thought, the schema-free approach of DocumentDB also makes it an excellent candidate for a CMS system.

Every user is reflected in a single document that describes all user preferences. The list of preferences can be easily extended by adding information to the document. Consider that users authenticate at an authentication service, for example, Azure Active Directory, Facebook, or Twitter, and that these services return a claim set, including a unique identifier called **nameidentifier**. This field is an excellent candidate for providing the unique entry point in our DocumentDB system and retrieving the user's profile information after logging in.

Logging information

A well-designed system usually emits logging information in large quantities and contains different types of information. Logging information is straightforward and contains information about a specific event, for example, a user logging in to the system, an exception raised by the system, or an audit trail record that needs to be persisted.

Because DocumentDB automatically indexes all documents, querying data and finding fault causes can be very quick. You can take DocumentDB information offline and store it in a datacenter for further analysis with tools like Hadoop or Power BI.

Building mobile solutions

Building and releasing mobile solutions is tough because we might have millions of customers. Using a schema-free database, it is easier to release new apps with additional data while still being able to service your old versions as well. Remember the troubles we had releasing a new schema of our SQL Server or Oracle database? Adding new tables and columns because of new features, and writing conversion scripts for every new release of the system?

By using a JSON document, we can easily add or remove information, release at a faster pace, and enable development in sprints—changing the data each sprint without the pain of conversion scripts.

Of course, the powerful scaling of DocumentDB is also a great help when building global, mobile apps servicing millions of users!

Exploring the data model

The internals of DocumentDB can themselves be described in a JSON document itself. The following figure displays a hierarchy of DocumentDB and its entities. This is called the DocumentDB **resource model** and all the entities are called resources.

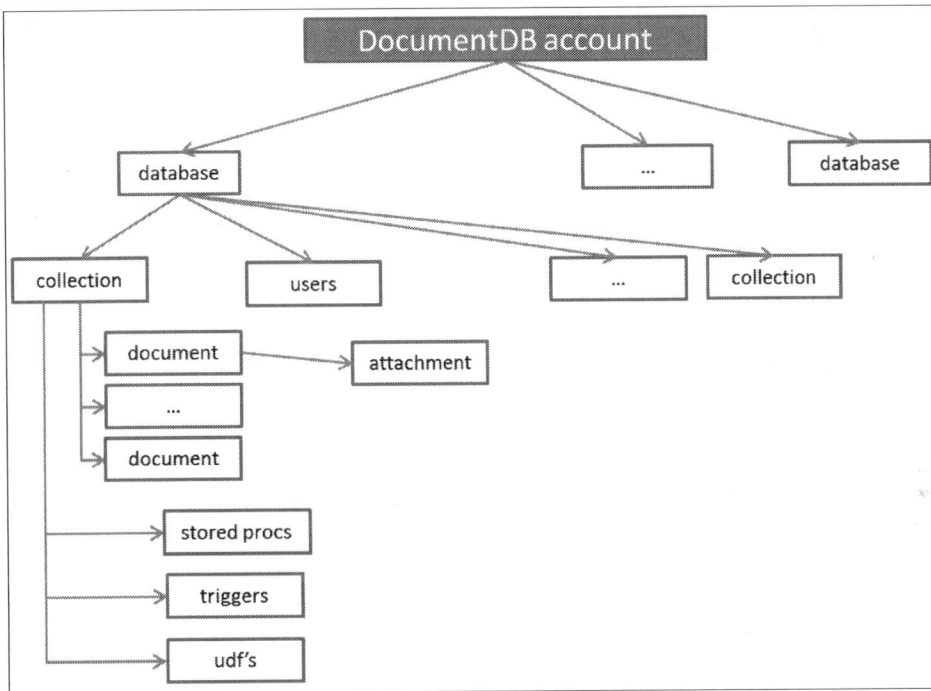

DocumentDB account

The main entry point is obviously a DocumentDB account. You need to have an account before you can start working with it. An account can contain databases and, as part of a preview feature, an amount of blob storage for attachments.

All resources are accessible through a logical URI, for example, the database with the name `persons` can be addressed through the logical URI `/dbs/persons` and the document describing the person John Doe, which has an ID of `12345`, can be addressed by the local URI `/dbs/persons/<collectionid>/docs/12345`.

Creating databases

A database is a container where documents are stored inside collections. Part of the database also forms a user's container. The user's container has a set of permissions, and the permissions to access collections, UDFs, triggers and SP are set on a database level. We can grant access to users in a fine-grained manner for accessing collections and documents.

A database is scaled elastically and does not need any interference from the account owner. It can scale from megabytes to petabytes. The data is stored on an SSD disk, providing fast access to your documents.

Databases are spanned implicitly across different underlying machines in order to provide the level of scaling we need.

Administering users

A user stored in DocumentDB is an abstraction of the concept user. A user is not a person logging in, but a set of permissions. Eventually, a DocumentDB user can be mapped to an Active Directory user or some third-party identity management system.

A simple, straightforward way of designing the user model is to create exactly one user per tenant or customer. That user only has permission to access collections and documents inside one database. This is the database belonging to the designated tenant and/or customer. This is a flat user model, but it is also possible to create user identities corresponding to actual users representing certain personas. This can give you more fine-grained control but will also increase the burden of user administration.

Users can be managed through the Azure portal (`portal.azure.com`) and also via the rich REST API or client SDKs that are provided by Microsoft.

Setting permissions

Implicitly, DocumentDB contains two types of roles: an administrator and a user. The administrator is the one that has the permission to manage and manipulate database accounts, databases, users, and permissions. These are considered the *administrative resources*, analogous to the metadata describing the full DocumentDB ecosystem. The administrator is provided with a *master key*. The master key is part of the DocumentDB account and is provided to the one setting up the account.

A user, on the other hand, is the person who manipulates actual data inside collections and documents, or changes UDFs (*application resources*). A user gets a *resource key* that provides access to specific application resources like databases and collections.

Managing collections

A collection can be described as a container for all the documents, but it is also a *unit of scale*. Adding collections will result in some SSD storage to be allocated for that particular collection. As we saw before, setting the performance level is done on a collection level. Inside your database, you can have multiple collections, each having their own performance level (S1, S2, or S3). For example, we could have a `UserProfile` collection containing documents with specific profile information like addresses, images, UI preferences, and so on. This collection is queried once a user logs in to your system and the profile information is retrieved from the `UserProfile` collection. Imagine we have another collection containing all the products that can be ordered. This collection will be accessed more frequently, hopefully, and therefore we can set an S3 level on this collection to provide the best performance for our potential buyers.

Collections grow and shrink implicitly when documents are added or removed. There is no need to allocate space or do other preconfiguration steps.

DocumentDB versus other databases

This section compares DocumentDB with other (non-)SQL technologies. The comparison is made with MongoDB and Azure Table storage.

Azure Table storage

Table storage is a non-SQL tabular based storage mechanism enabling you to store rows and columns inside a table. A table is not fixed, meaning that different rows can have different columns. Azure Table storage is a perfect fit for storing large amounts of data, although it is non-relational. There are no mechanisms like foreign keys, triggers, or user-defined functions.

MongoDB

MongoDB is also a document database (NoSQL), which means that it is schema-free, enables high performance and high availability, and has the ability to scale. MongoDB is open source, and is built around documents and collections. The documents are compiled of sets of key-value pairs, while collections also contain documents. Compared to DocumentDB, MongoDB uses BSON instead of JSON.

Comparison chart

The following table provides a high-level comparison on some key features:

Feature	DocumentDB	MongoDB	Table storage
Model	Document	Document	Rows and columns
Database schema	Schema-free	Schema-free	Schema-free
Triggers	Yes	No	No
Server side scripts	Yes, JavaScript	Yes, JavaScript	No
Foreign keys	*N/A	N/A	N/A
Indexing	Potentially on property	Potentially on every property	Partition key and row key only
Transactions	Yes, supports ACID	No	Limited, using batching
Hosting	On Microsoft Azure only, offered as a service	Can be on-premise or on a virtual machine, not offered as a service	On Microsoft Azure, offered as a service.

DocumentDB does not offer referential integrity by design. There is no concept of foreign keys. Integrity can be enforced by using triggers and SPs.

The role of the Database Administrator is still needed to manage DocumentDB. We still need someone to overlook our databases and collections. Some common tasks a DBA for a document might perform are as follows:

- Creating and managing databases
- Creating and managing collections
- Getting responsibility on scaling, partitioning, and sharding
- Defining and maintaining SPs, user-defined functions, and triggers
- Managing users and permissions
- Measuring performance

Understanding the price model

This section provides a brief overview of how your bill is influenced by the way you use DocumentDB. There are a few factors that determine the pricing:

- Having a DocumentDB account
- Number of collections inside a database
- Performance level
- Capacity units

Account charges

When you set up a DocumentDB account, you will be billed immediately. An empty account with no databases and hence no collections will be charged for a single S1 collection, at around $25 per month. The reason that you are charged while not having any collections or documents is that Microsoft needs to reserve a DNS and authorization scope for the account.

Number of collections

Collections are billed by the hour. Having a collection for only 10 minutes will still incur charges for a whole hour. An amount of 10 GB is included for all tiers.

The following table defines the standard characteristics per performance level:

Performance level	SSD storage	Request units	Price per hour
S1	10 GB	250 per second	$0.034
S2	10 GB	1,000 per second	$0.067
S3	10 GB	2,500 per second	$0.134

Request units are calculated based on the amount of resources that are needed for the operation performed. When more CPU, IO, and memory is needed for a certain operation, more request units are calculated. The number of request units needed for each operation is returned in the response's header (x-ms-request-charge). By reading this value, you can keep track of the usage. If you exceed the number of request units, additional operations will be throttled.

To have fine-grained control over the performance of your collections, you could do the housekeeping of consumed **Requests Units (RUs)** yourself and check if you often exceed the maximum number of RUs. If so, upgrading the performance level for your collection might be a good idea.

> It is possible to upgrade and downgrade a collection from S1 to S2 or S3, but the charges are for the highest tier. Switching from S1 to S3 within 1 hour will therefore be billed at $0.134.

Request Units

The number of RUs needed for an operation depends on the following factors:

- **Size of the document**: Larger documents increase the consumption of RUs.

- **Number of properties**: More properties increase the consumption of RUs. When you use data consistency (we will dive into this concept later on), more RUs will be consumed.

- **Indexes**: When more properties are indexed, more RUs are needed. It is good practice to investigate the actual indexes you need for you scenario. Also, documents are indexed by default; turning this feature off will save RUs. SP and triggers also consume RUs based on the metrics mentioned previously.

Understanding storage

By default, a collection is provisioned with 10 GB of storage. Documents consume storage space, but indexes also fill up the space of a collection. If you need more storage space, you need to create a different collection.

Expanding resources

Microsoft offers the ability to contact Azure support from the Azure blade portal (portal.azure.com). If you need specific adjustments that you cannot manage from the portal or that are not supported by default, contact Azure support.

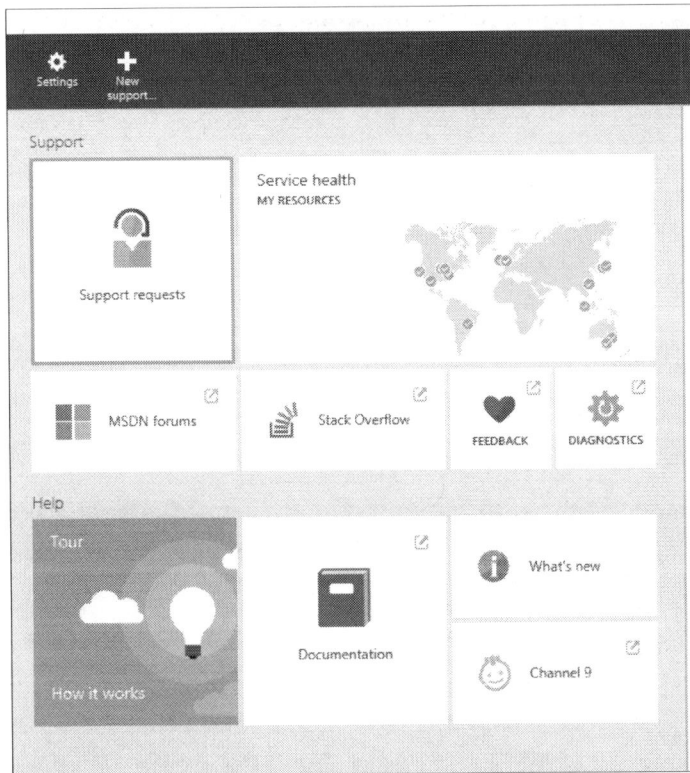

Click on the **New Support** button and follow the wizard that shows up. Make sure you choose the **Quotas** request type and enter your request details. The following table shows the limits that can be stretched by Azure support:

Database accounts	5
Number of SPs, triggers and UDFs per collection	25 each
Maximum collections per database account	100
Maximum document storage per database (100 collections)	1 TB
Maximum number of UDFs per query	1
Maximum number of JOINs per query	2
Maximum number of AND clauses per query	5
Maximum number of OR clauses per query	5
Maximum number of values per IN expression	100
Maximum number of collection created per minute	5

Building your first application

This paragraph provides a step-by-step approach to building a console application using Visual Studio 2015 that utilizes the basics of DocumentDB. We will perform the following steps:

1. Create a DocumentDB account.

2. Create a database.

3. Create a collection.

4. Build a console application that connects to DocumentDB and saves a document.

Provisioning an account

To create a DocumentDB account, you need to go to the Microsoft Azure portal. If you don't have a Microsoft Azure account yet, you can get a trial version at `https://azure.microsoft.com/en-us/pricing/free-trial/`.

After logging in to the Azure portal, go ahead and create your first DocumentDB account. For now, you only need to come up with a name.

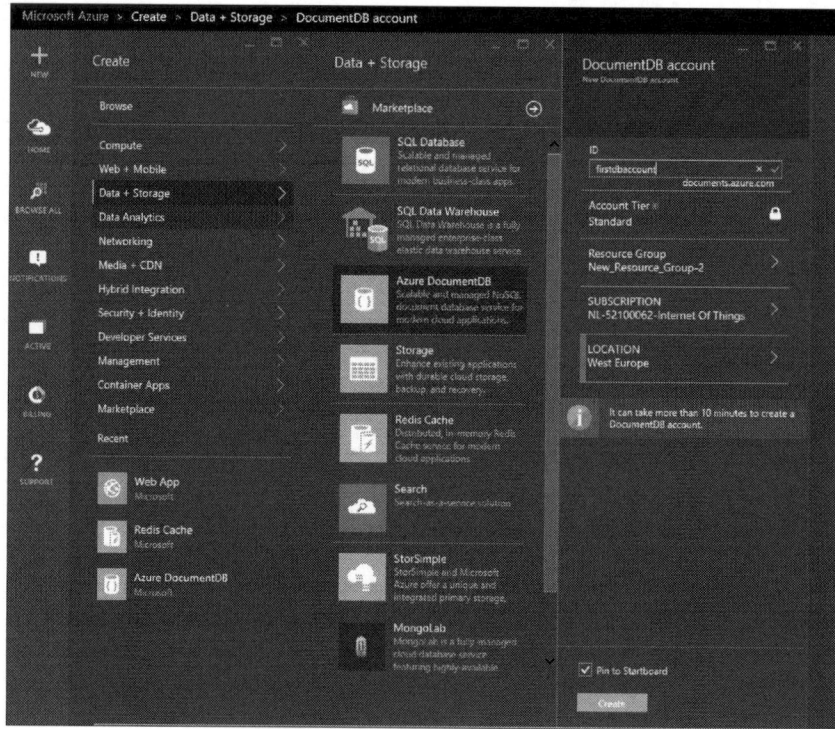

After clicking on the **Create** button, your DocumentDB account will be provisioned. This process might take some time to finish.

After provisioning, your account is ready for use. Select the account you have just created and you will get an overview.

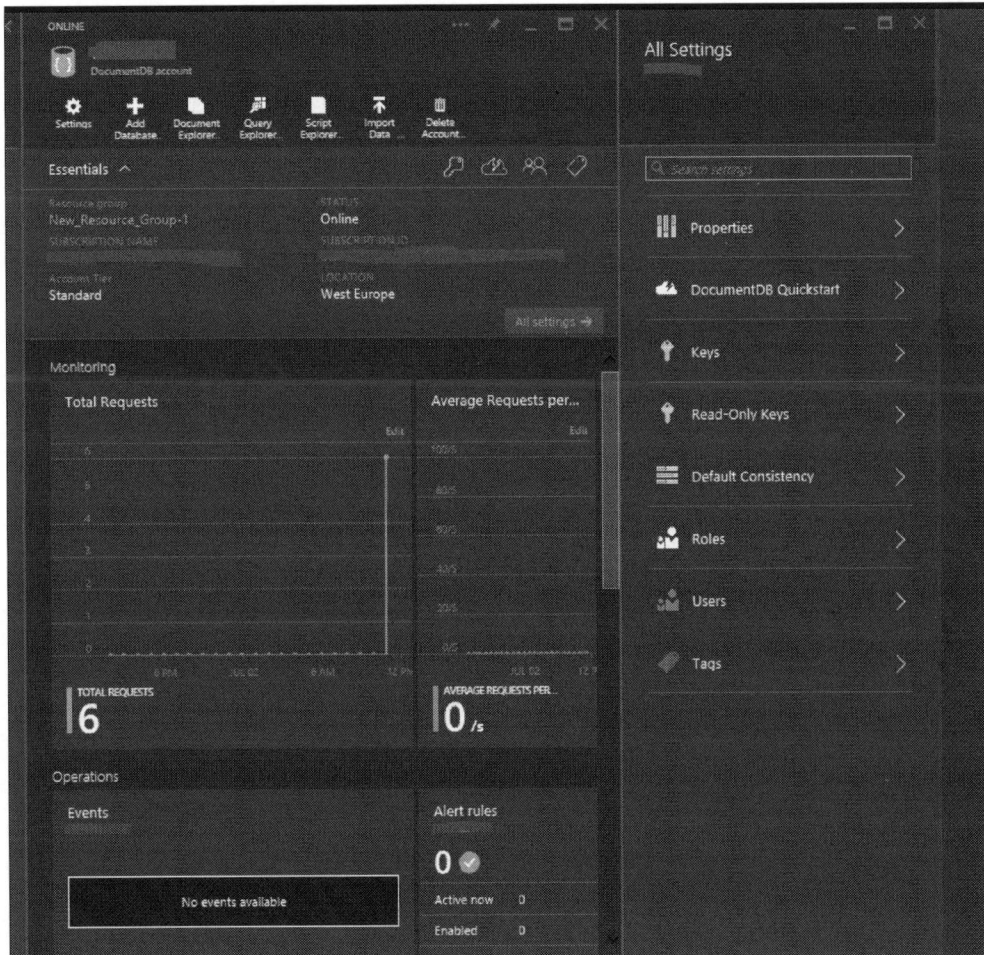

On the overview blade of your account, you will see a lot of information. For now, the most important information is located in the settings blade on the right-hand side. From this blade, you can retrieve keys and a connection string. We need this information if we want to start building the console application. Select the **DocumentDB** option, copy the URI, and copy the primary key.

Creating a database

In order to be able to create collections, we need a database first. Creating a database is straightforward as it only needs a name as input. Click the **Add Database** button and enter a meaningful name. After selecting **OK**, your database is provisioned. On the left blade you can scroll down and locate your new database.

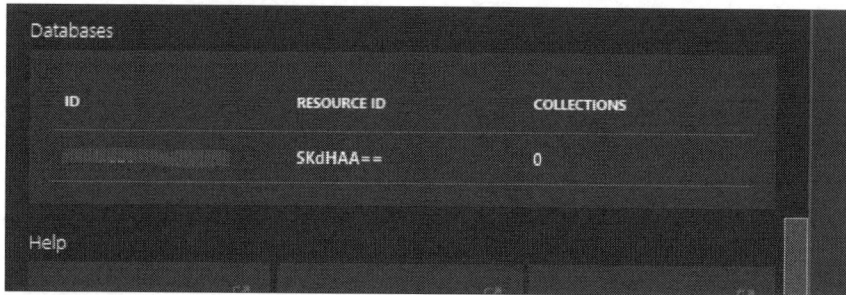

Creating a collection

As we have seen before, a collection is created inside a database. Selecting your database gives you the ability to add a collection. When the **Add Collection** option is selected, you need to pick the right performance level (or tier). For this demo, the **S1** tier is more than sufficient.

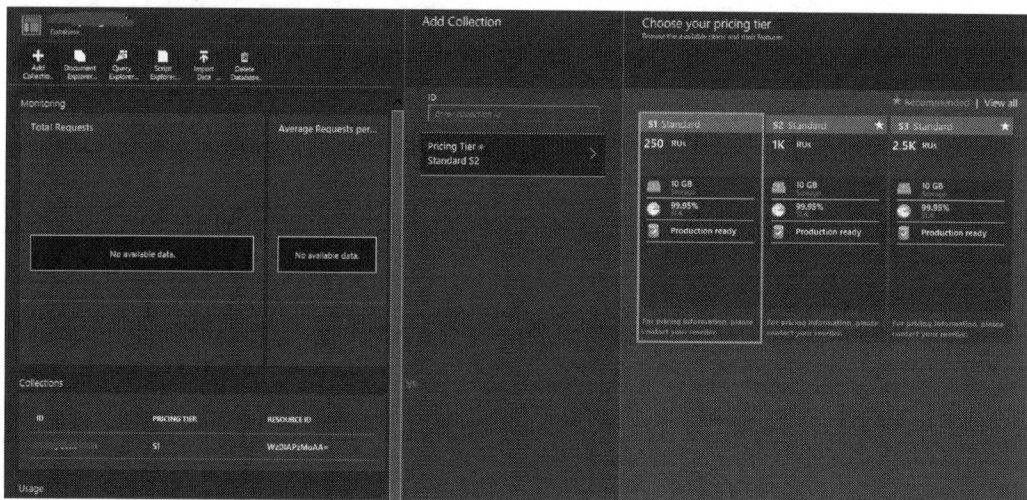

Now that we have our DocumentDB account, a database, and a collection, we can start building our first application.

> Creating databases and collections can also be done through the REST API or the designated SDKs.

Building a console application

This sample is built using Visual Studio 2015. If you do not have Visual Studio 2015, you can download the free version Visual Studio 2015 Community from `https://www.visualstudio.com/en-us/products/visual-studio-express-vs.aspx`.

Setting up a solution

Here are the steps for creating a Visual Studio solution containing a console application that will demonstrate the basic usage of DocumentDB:

1. Start Visual Studio.

2. Go to **File | New Project** and then click on the **Console Application** template.

3. Name your project `MyFirstDocDbApp`.

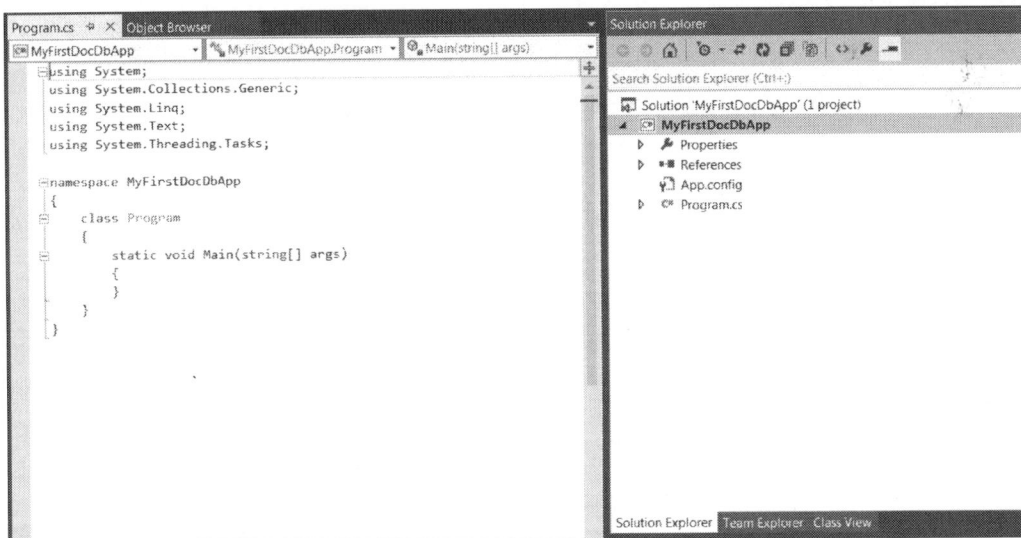

Visual Studio now creates a console application.

4. In order to work with DocumentDB, we need to pull in a NuGet package. Right-click on your project file and select **Manage NuGet Packages**. Search for the **Microsoft Azure DocumentDB Client Library**.

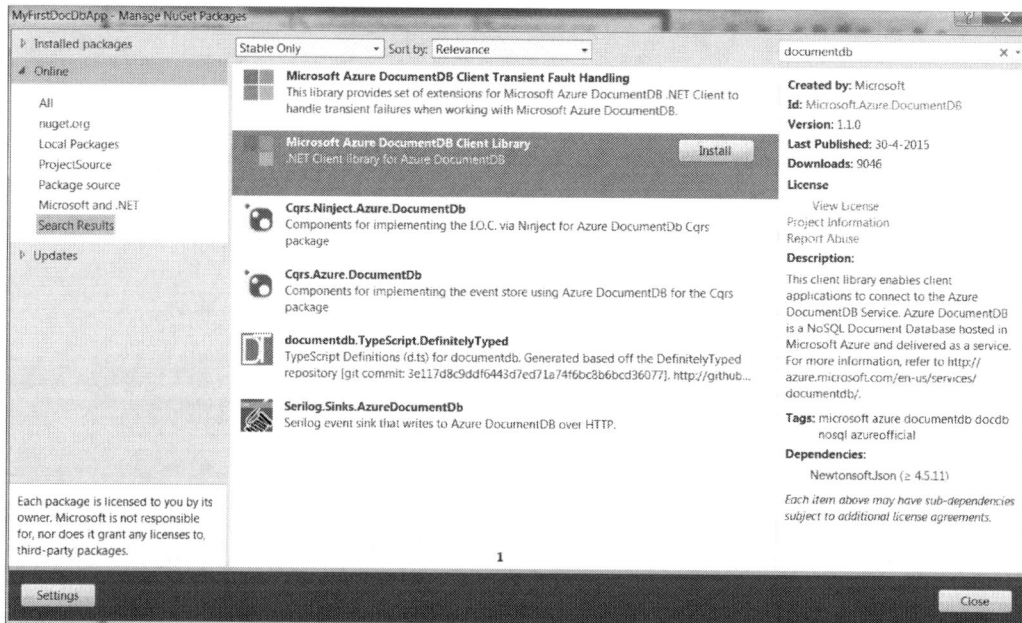

5. Select the right package in the search results and click **Install**. Your project is now ready to use the DocumentDB Client Library.

Saving a document

Now that we have set up a solution, created a project, and enabled the right .NET library to manage DocumentDB, we are going to write some C# code.

> Keep in mind that although the code samples in this book are mostly in C#, you can also use the programming language of your choice. There are SDKs available for multiple platforms (Java, Python, Node.js, and JavaScript). If yours is not supported, you could always use the REST API.

*   Add the following `using` statements to the top of the `program.cs` file:

```
using Microsoft.Azure.Documents;
using Microsoft.Azure.Documents.Client;
using Microsoft.Azure.Documents.Linq;
using Newtonsoft.Json;
```

- We need the URI and primary key that we retrieved in the previous paragraph.

After writing a few lines of C# code, we have the code snippet ready. It performs the following tasks:

- Makes a connection to the DocumentDB account
- Finds the database that is created in the portal
- Creates a collection named `testdevicehub`
- Saves a document to this collection

The code is as follows:

```
private static async Task CreateDocument()
  {
    //attach to DocumentDB using the URI and Key from the Azure
      portal
    DocumentClient client = new DocumentClient(new Uri(docDBUri),
      key);
    //query for the right database inside the DocDB account
    Database database = client.CreateDatabaseQuery().Where(d =>
      d.Id == "devicehub").AsEnumerable().FirstOrDefault();
    //find the right collection where we want to add the document
    DocumentCollection collection =
      client.CreateDocumentCollectionQuery(
      (String)database.SelfLink).
        ToList().Where(cl => cl.Id.Equals(
          "testdevicehub")).FirstOrDefault();
    //create a simple document in the collection by providing the
      DocumentsLink and the object to be serialized
    //and stored
    await client.CreateDocumentAsync(
      collection.DocumentsLink,
      new PersonInformation
      {
        FirstName = "Riccardo",
        LastName = "Becker",
        DateOfBirth = new DateTime(1974, 12, 21)
      }
    );
  }
```

Replace the values of `docDBUri` and the key with your information and run the console application. You have just created your first document.

Now, go to the Azure portal again and open the query documents screen. You need to select the designated collection to enable this option. Running the base query returns the document that we have just created:

```
select * from c
```

Here's the screenshot:

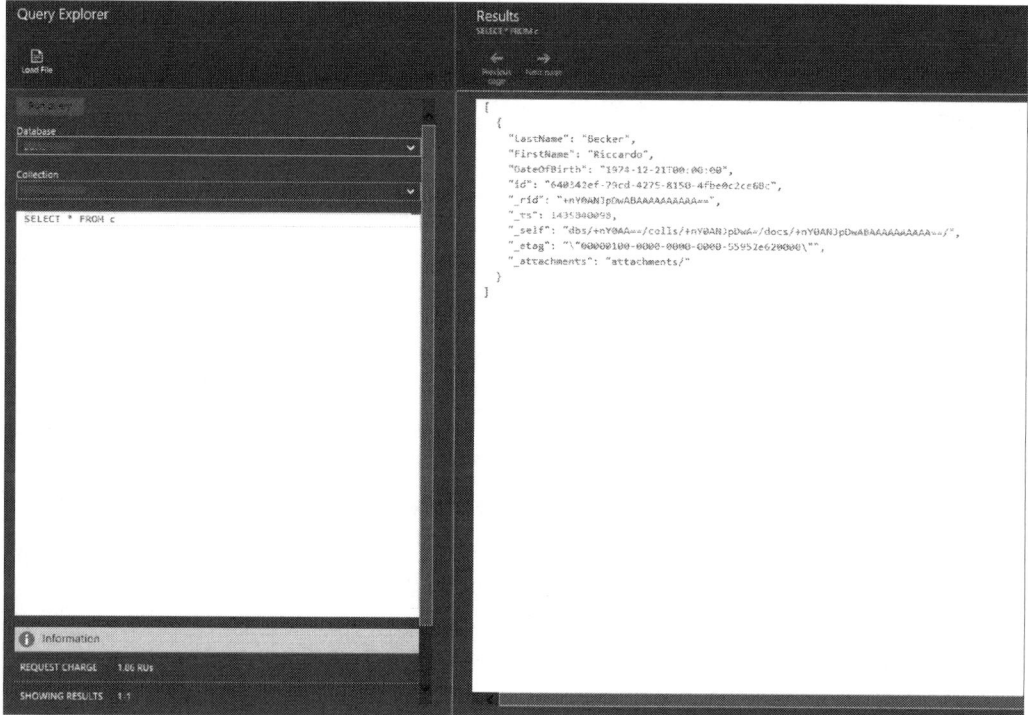

As you can see, the document contains more than just the fields from the class `PersonInformation`. Here is a brief explanation of these fields:

- `id`: This is the unique identifier for the document. In the application we have just created, the ID is automatically generated and is represented by a GUID.
- `_rid`: This resource ID is an internally used property.
- `_ts`: This is a property generated by the system, and it contains a timestamp.

- `_self`: This is generated by the system, and it contains a unique URI pointing to this resource document.

- `_etag`: This is a system-generated property containing an `ETag` that can be used for optimistic concurrency scenarios (if somebody updates the same document in the meantime, the `ETag` will differ and your update will fail).

- `_attachments`: This is generated by the system, and it contains the path for the attachments resource belonging to this document.

Summary

In this chapter, we covered the basics of DocumentDB. We saw that we can literally store *everything* and there is no predefined schema we need to comply with. The Azure portal offers some interesting blades for us to create, configure, and manage DocumentDB resources and offers some quick-starts to help you get started immediately. The internals of DocumentDB were discussed and we got a nice insight of the data model.

We also saw some common use cases that are applicable for DocumentDB. A small section was dedicated to explain the pricing model and how your bill is affected by actions you can do.

Finally, we started to do a bit of coding and wrote a small C# console application that connects to the database and creates a document. We could see in the Azure portal that the document was actually stored, together with some other interesting metadata.

In the next chapter, we will discuss how to manage and monitor your DocumentDB resources.

2
Setting up and Managing Your Database

Besides programming against a database, it is also of utmost importance that your database is well managed. You can manage a database not only from the portal, but also using the REST API's or the different client SDKs.

In this chapter, we will cover the following topics:

- Managing and regenerating keys
- Creating resource tokens
- Learning about consistency levels
- Viewing and setting performance and usage metrics
- Setting up alerts and seeing them in action

Managing your keys

As we have seen in *Chapter 1, Getting Started with DocumentDB*, access to your databases is granted by a combination of the URI to your DocumentDB and a key. In the Azure portal, on the **All Settings** blade of your database, you can see both your primary and secondary keys. Both keys can be used to access your database. But why are there two keys?

Recycling keys

DocumentDB, like other persistency mechanisms on Azure, such as Table storage, provides two keys. This is because it is good practice to regenerate your keys periodically to keep your connections more secure. The two-key approach enables access to your database with one key while regenerating the other. This way, your application is always online, while the keys are changed on a regular basis. This process is called *rolling your keys*.

Perform the following steps to roll your keys:

1. Update all your applications that are using the primary key to use the secondary key.

2. Regenerate the primary key from the Azure portal.

> Clicking on **Regenerate Primary** will result in a new primary key for your database. Remember, all applications using this primary key cannot connect to your database from now on, so plan this carefully and make sure they are using the secondary key.

3. When the new primary key is available (this process takes a few minutes), update all your applications again to use this new primary key.

4. The last step is to regenerate the secondary key as well.

Storing keys in your application configuration files is generally bad practice. In *Chapter 7, Advanced Techniques*, we will see how to use different approaches that enable a higher security level for your application, for example, by using Azure Key Vault.

> Azure Key Vault enables you to store sensitive keys in a central place. These keys are protected by hardware security modules and offer a high level of security.

Managing read-only keys

In the previous screenshot, you can also find the option to manage your read-only keys. Why are these keys available and how should these be used?

Imagine providing the primary or secondary key to applications inside your company (or even outside it in a SaaS-like application). Sharing these keys is a very bad idea, since it will give everybody administrative privileges and manage your database for you. Read-only keys are there to provide read-only access to your database and all its resources. System administrators of your customers or departments might be good candidates for this. There is a more fine-grained way of providing access to specific resources in your database — resource tokens.

Using resource tokens

Resource tokens are tokens associated with permission resources and establish connections between a user and the permissions of that user for resources stored in DocumentDB (collections, documents, and stored procedures).

Creating resource tokens

Imagine a scenario where a multi-tenant web application needs access to your database. For each tenant, a separate collection inside the database is created. The web application only needs access to the specific collection for the tenant. We can solve this by creating a resource token only for the new collection.

The following steps are performed to achieve this goal:

1. Create a tenant-specific collection.
2. Create a resource token for that collection.
3. Have the web application use the resource token to gain access to the collection.

Creating a collection

The following C# code snippet creates a collection for a tenant called `Contoso`:

```
// Check if collection already exists
DocumentCollection tenantCollection =
client.CreateDocumentCollectionQuery(database.CollectionsLink)
.Where(c => c.Id == TenantName)
.AsEnumerable()
.FirstOrDefault();

if (tenantCollection == null)
{
  // Create collection
  tenantCollection = await client.CreateDocumentCollectionAsync(
    database.CollectionsLink,
    new DocumentCollection { Id = TenantName });
}
```

After running this code, the collection is created with the name **Contoso**. You can check this in the Azure portal. It shows that the **Contoso** collection exists in the **deviceHub** database.

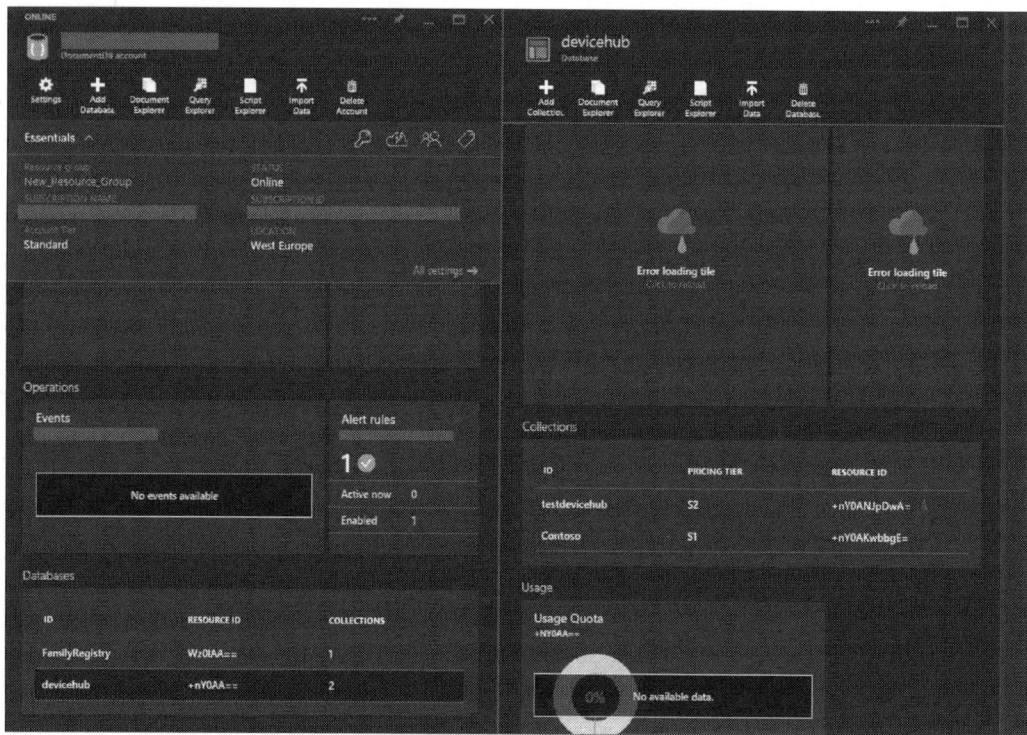

Creating a user and its permission

Now that we have the collection available, it is time to create a user and permissions for the **Contoso** collection.

The following C# code snippet creates a user and a permission for the **Contoso** collection. It also shows how to query for existing users and permissions. If the user already exists, simply ignore it. The code is as follows:

```
User readUser = new User
{
  Id = TenantName + "ReadUser"
};
try
{
  //Create a user and check if it does not exist already
  docUser = client.CreateUserQuery("dbs/" + database.ResourceId
    + "/users/").AsEnumerable().Where(u => u.Id == docUser.Id)
    .FirstOrDefault();
  if (docUser == null)
  {
    docUser = await client.CreateUserAsync(database.SelfLink,
      docUser);
  }
  //create another user called readUser, omitted in the snippet


  Permission collectionPermission = new Permission
  {
    PermissionMode = PermissionMode.All, //give all permissions
    ResourceLink = tenantCollection.SelfLink,
    Id = "allPermissions"
  };
  //now create the permission for the docUser if it does not
    exist yet
  try
  {
    collectionPermission = client.CreatePermissionQuery("/dbs/"
      + database.ResourceId + "/users/" + docUser.ResourceId +
      "/permissions").
    AsEnumerable().Where(u => u.Id ==
      collectionPermission.Id).FirstOrDefault();
    if (collectionPermission == null)
    {
```

```
        collectionPermission = await client
          .CreatePermissionAsync(docUser.SelfLink,
          collectionPermission);
      }
    }
```

This code snippet creates a new user called `Contoso_User` and creates an `All` permission for it on the **Contoso** collection. With this permission, the user can manage the whole collection, add documents, modify them, and delete them (and of course, add stored procedures, user-defined functions, and so on). It also creates a read-only permission.

> Remember that resource permissions are valid for only 1 hour by default. You can override this and set it to a maximum of 5 hours.

The permission we have just created will only last for 1 hour by default. The `collectionPermission` and `readOnlyCollectionPermission` variables contain a token that can be used to create a `documentClient`. This is all contained in the code project that belongs to this chapter.

Creating a document with permissions

In this code snippet, we will see how the `collectionPermission` variable can be used to add a document to the collection:

```
DocumentClient manageClient = new DocumentClient(new
  Uri(docDBUri), collectionPermission.Token);

//now see if we can add a document
try
{
ResourceResponse<Document> response = await
  manageClient.CreateDocumentAsync(
  tenantCollection.DocumentsLink,
  new PersonInformation
  {
    FirstName = "Riccardo",
    LastName = "Becker",
    DateOfBirth = new DateTime(1974, 12, 21)
  }
  );
```

```
    }
    catch (DocumentClientException de)
    {
      //we should not get here
      if (de.StatusCode != HttpStatusCode.Unauthorized)
      {
        throw;
      }
    }
```

The `CreateDocumentAsync` function is successful and the response contains information about the document we have just created. The `DocumentClientException` variable is not raised.

Creating a document without permissions

Using the `readonly` permission, we can create a document and throw the `Unauthorized` exception:

```
DocumentClient readonlyClient = new DocumentClient(new Uri(docDBUri),
readOnlyCollectionPermission.Token);

    //now see if we can add a document, this should fail!
    try
    {
      await readonlyClient.CreateDocumentAsync(
      tenantCollection.DocumentsLink,
      new PersonInformation
      {
        FirstName = "John",
        LastName = "Doe",
        DateOfBirth = new DateTime(1975, 1, 1)
      }
      );
    }
    catch (DocumentClientException de)
    {
      //we SHOULD get here
      if (de.StatusCode != HttpStatusCode.Unauthorized)
      {
        Console.WriteLine("A valid exception!");
      }
    }
```

The `CreateDocumentAsync` function is not successful and the `DocumentClientException` is raised. The `readonlyCollectionPermission` token is not authorized to create a document.

These code snippets contain a short version. The full project is provided and is capable of running multiple times without throwing exceptions of already existing resources.

In the Azure portal, we can verify that only one additional document is created inside the **Contoso** collection.

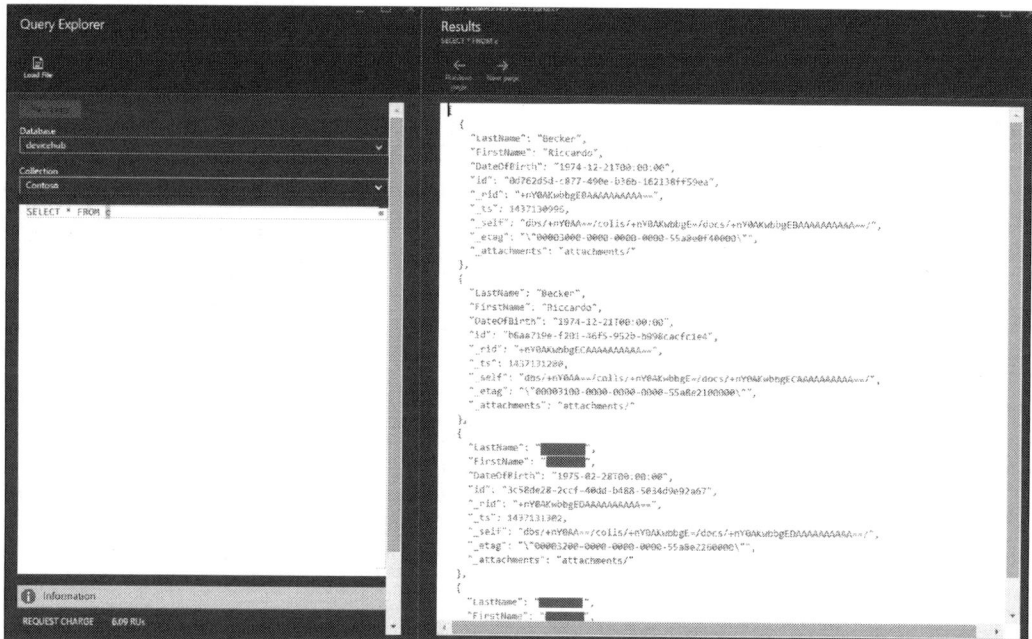

It is interesting to see the amount of RUs that are used for this specific query to list all documents inside our **Contoso** collection. Running the same query multiple times results in different numbers of RUs being charged, because it is based on CPU and IO (which is hard to predict from our side).

Listing permissions

The following code snippet will get all the permissions of a user inside your database:

```
User user = await client.ReadUserAsync(readUser.SelfLink);

    FeedResponse<Permission> permissions = await
      client.ReadPermissionFeedAsync(readUser.SelfLink);
    foreach (var permission in permissions)
    {
      Console.WriteLine(permission.Id + ":" +
        permission.ResourceLink + ":" +
        permission.PermissionMode.ToString());
    }
```

Setting consistency levels

Consistency levels are settings on the account level of DocumentDB. This means that setting a consistency level reflects all your assets, including databases and collections. Setting consistency levels affects performance, so choose wisely. There are four consistency levels you can choose from:

- **STRONG**: A write transaction is only visible after it has been committed to all replicas. Uncommitted or partial write actions are never seen by any client. This means that a user only sees the latest committed write. Strong consistency provides a guarantee on consistency (as its name implies) but offers the lowest read and/or write performance.

- **SESSION**: This level is bound to the session of a client. This means that both reads and writes have low latency, because they are performed on the specific client version of the data.

- **BOUNDED**: Bounded consistency guarantees the total order of propagation of writes. This means that reads lag behind writes and reading data means you get the data that is offered by the majority of replicas. This level offers predictable behavior on read consistency but offers the lowest latency writes. Since reading is determined by the majority of replicas, this level offers a better read performance than **STRONG**.

- **EVENTUAL**: This Provides the weakest form of consistency because it is not certain that reading gets the latest values. Eventually, the replicas will converge and provide the same data but the point in time is non-deterministic. This level of consistency is the weakest but it offers the lowest latency.

Consistency levels can be set inside the Azure portal, as shown in the following screenshot:

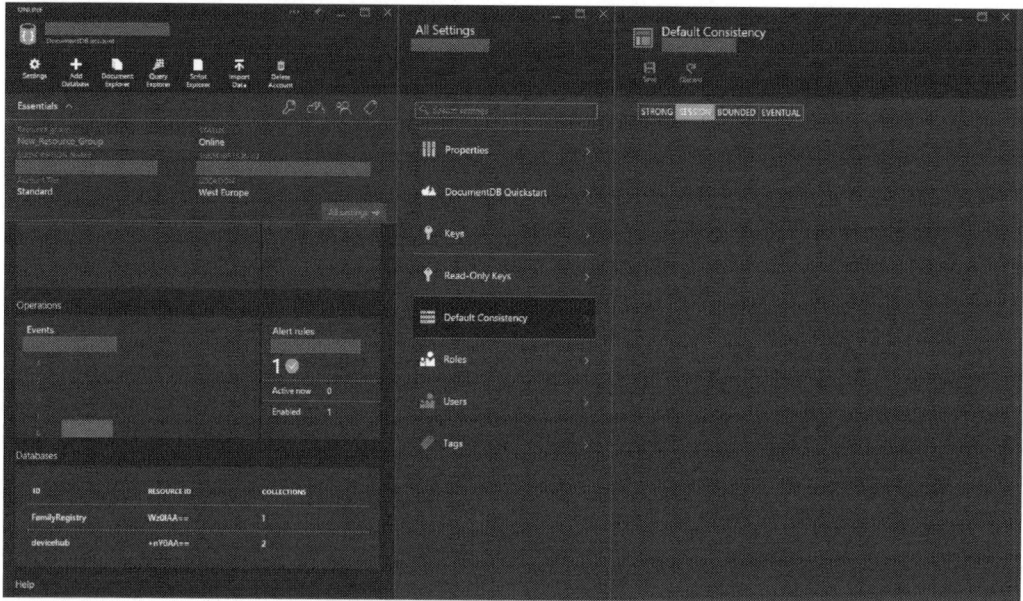

Managing alerts

In this section, we will learn how to monitor your assets, gather metrics, and create alerts.

Monitoring your account

The Azure portal offers the ability to monitor your account. There are performance metrics and usage metrics available for you to view.

Selecting the monitoring lens will bring up the details of your monitoring settings.

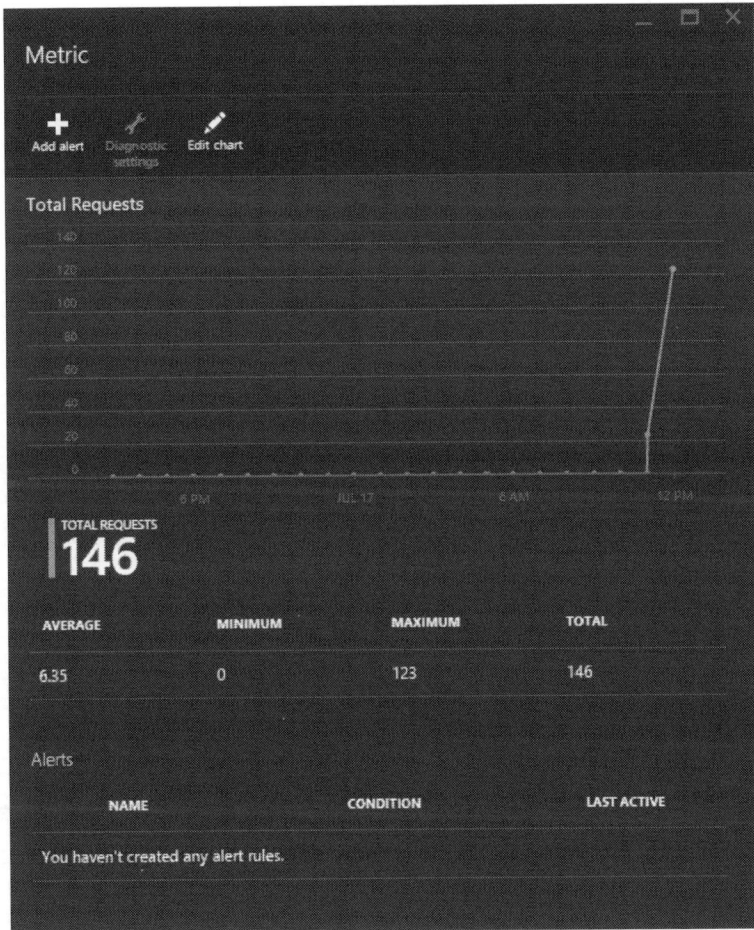

By default, you will see the amount of total requests on your account. By selecting the **Edit chart** option, we can add multiple metrics to our chart. Selecting the **today** time range and checking all the available metrics will give you a detailed overview of all the events that happened today on the account.

Other possible metrics to add are shown in the following screenshot:

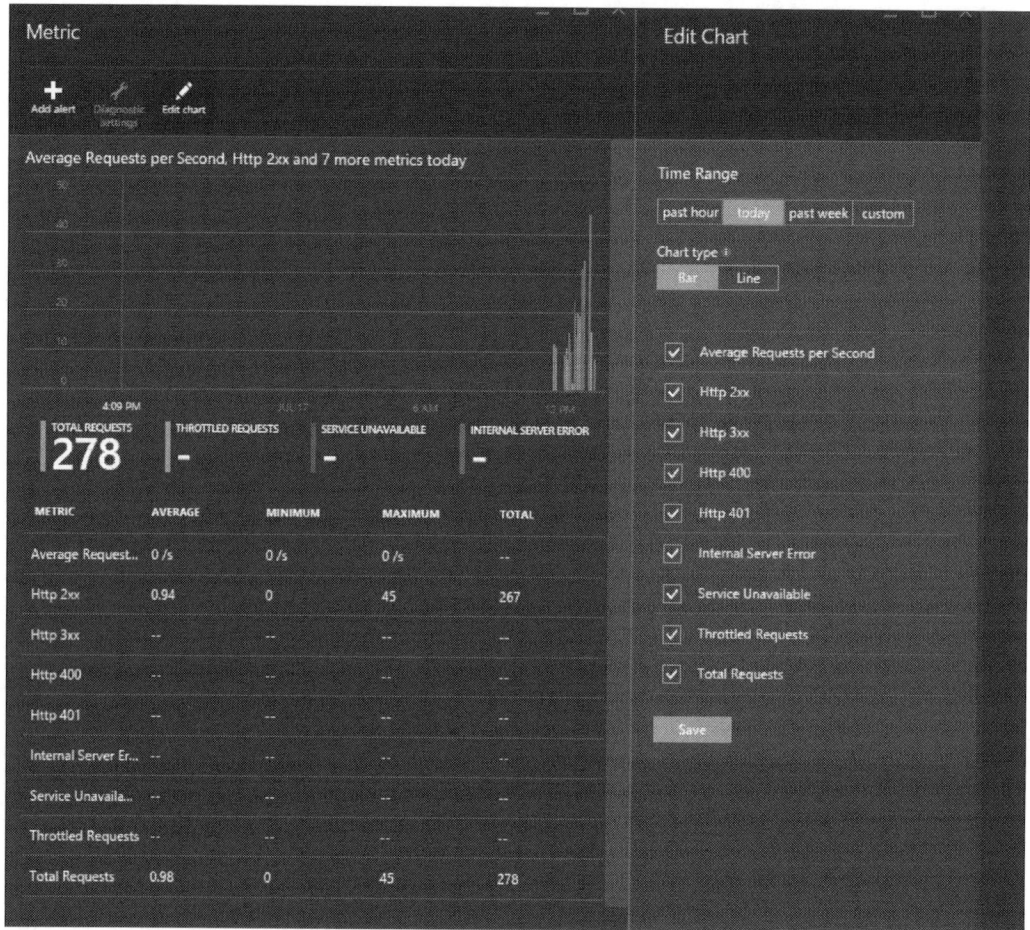

> All metrics are interesting, but pay close attention to the **Http 401** because it indicates the amount of unauthorized requests. This might be due to permissions expiring or worse, a possible attack on your system.

Creating alerts

Inside the same blade, we can create alerts. Select the **Add alert** option and fill out the alert settings, as shown in the following screenshot:

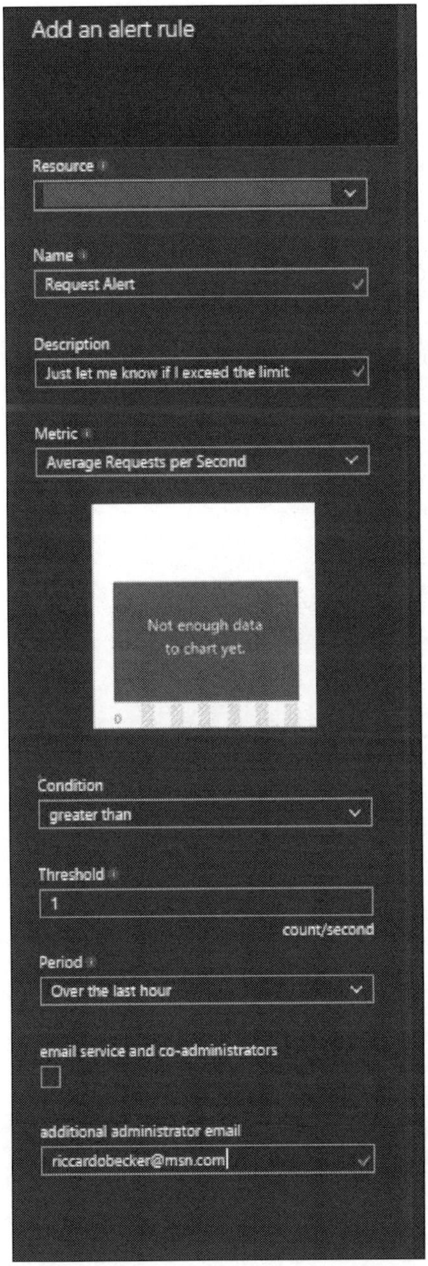

> It takes quite some effort to activate this alert, since Azure will provision resources in the datacenter to enable this feature. Starting the application several times will help to activate the alert.

The alert we have created here is based on the **Average Requests per second** metric. If this exceeds the threshold of 1 per second in the last hour, we want to be notified. In this case, an e-mail is sent to my e-mail account, telling me that a threshold has been exceeded.

Summary

In this chapter, we discussed how to manage and regenerate the different keys of your database. We also covered how to manage permissions on a resource level. We talked about consistency levels of your DocumentDB account, how they can affect the consistency of your data, and how they can affect the performance. The second part of the chapter explained how to create alerts on your database and how to manage these inside the Azure portal.

In the next chapter, we will cover the basics of querying your databases.

3
Basic Querying

This chapter will guide you through the processes of creating, reading, updating, and deleting resources in your database (CRUD operations). We will focus on collections, documents, and users. Each section will discuss how to achieve these CRUD operations on the different resource types, with real code examples.

In this chapter, we will cover:

- Concepts of CRUD operations inside DocumentDB
- Different operations on collections, users, and documents
- Building a C# program that demonstrates and explains the CRUD operations

Creating resources

As we have seen before, entities inside DocumentDB are called resources. The way resources are managed is a uniform process, and this makes understanding these CRUD operations easier. This section will discuss how to create resources inside your database.

Creating a collection

Before you can create and update documents, you first need to have a collection available. In *Chapter 1, Getting Started with DocumentDB*, we saw how a collection can be created straight from the Azure portal. In this section, we are going to create one by using the .NET SDK using Visual Studio 2013 and C#.

The following code snippet shows how you can check if a collection already exists; it also demonstrates how a collection can be created:

```
//prerequisite before we can work. We need a DocumentClient and a
  Database.
    DocumentClient client = new DocumentClient(new Uri(docDBUri),
key);
    Database database = client.CreateDatabaseQuery().Where(d =>
      d.Id == "devicehub").AsEnumerable().First();

    //create a collection for chapter 3, also check if it does not
      exist already.
    DocumentCollection collection =
      client.CreateDocumentCollectionQuery(database.SelfLink).
        Where(cl => cl.Id.Equals("chapter3"))
          .AsEnumerable().First();
      if (null == collection)
      {
        // go ahead and create one
        collection = await client
          .CreateDocumentCollectionAsync(database.SelfLink,
        new DocumentCollection
        {
          Id = "chapter3"
        });
      }
      //the collection exists.
```

The following figure shows a fragment from the Azure portal; the `chapter3` collection we have just created is there.

Collections		
ID	**PRICING TIER**	**RESOURCE ID**
testdevicehub	S2	+nY0ANJpDwA=
Contoso	S1	+nY0AKwbbgE=
chapter3	S1	+nY0AK1WiwE=

Creating a document

In *Chapter 1, Getting Started with DocumentDB*, we saw how a document can be created inside a collection. This section also demonstrates if the document to be created already exists. The code example demonstrates three ways of querying a collection for the existence of a document:

- **Using plain DocumentDB SQL**: This is a good way of demonstrating the SQL syntax but there is no type-safety using this method
- **Using LINQ to objects**: This can operate on a collection because it returns `IEnumerable` or `IEnumerable<T>`
- **Using LINQ**: Using standard LINQ queries to operate on your collections and documents.

Using DocumentDB SQL

DocumentDB offers an SQL-like capability to query documents. The following snippet shows how to write a `SELECT` statement:

```
//check if document exists using DocumentDB SQL
var documentBySql = client.CreateDocumentQuery(collection.
DocumentsLink,
"SELECT * " +
    "FROM chapter3 c " +
    "WHERE c.FirstName = \"Riccardo\" AND
    c.LastName= \"Becker\"").AsEnumerable().First();
```

This code snippet returns an object of type document. Using this object, we can easily delete from the collection by using the available `SelfLink` property.

Using LINQ to object

Besides writing plain SQL statements, DocumentDB also offers a LINQ interface. This LINQ provider is part of the .NET client library. The following snippet demonstrates how the same query can be written by using LINQ:

```
var documentByLinqToObjects = client.CreateDocumentQuery<PersonInforma
tion>(collection.DocumentsLink)
  .Where(personInformation => personInformation
   .FirstName.Equals("Riccardo")
  && personInformation.LastName.Equals(
    "Becker")).AsEnumerable<PersonInformation>().First();
```

Using LINQ

It is also possible to execute plain LINQ queries using inline clauses against your collection. The following snippet demonstrates how find a specific document with the `FirstName` and `LastName` properties:

```
//check if document already exists using Linq
var documentByLinq = (from c in client.CreateDocumentQuery<PersonInfor
mation>(collection.DocumentsLink)
   where c.FirstName.Equals("Riccardo")
   && c.LastName.Equals("Becker")
   select c).AsEnumerable<PersonInformation>().First();
```

Updating the PersonInformation

As we saw, the `SelfLink` property is important for building solutions using DocumentDB. When using LINQ to return a `PersonInformation` object from your collection, by default, it only contains the `FirstName`, `LastName`, and `DateOfBirth` properties. The plain old CLR object (POCO) `PersonInformation` needs some additional properties.

> To enable your POCOs to contain the `SelfLink` property, as well as other properties needed later on, derive your POCO from Resource!

In the following code snippet, we will see how it is possible to enable our `PersonInformation` POCO to contain the DocumentDB properties needed. Since every entity in DocumentDB is a resource, we derive from the `Resource` class:

```
public class PersonInformation : Resource
  {
    public string LastName { get; set; }
    public string FirstName { get; set; }
    public DateTime DateOfBirth { get; set; }
  }
```

Reading resources

Let's see how to perform some basic reading operations on your collection. We extend the `PersonInformation` class with more fields to be able to demonstrate some more detailed querying capabilities. The `PersonInformation` class now also contains a list of roles a person can have. This enables us to query on the `Roles` property as well.

The class is defined as follows:

```
public class PersonInformation : Resource
{
  public string LastName { get; set; }
  public string FirstName { get; set; }
  public DateTime DateOfBirth { get; set; }

  public List<Role> Roles { get; set; }
}

public class Role
{
  public string RoleName {get;set;}
}
```

Reading documents

In this section, we will use the Roles property of the PersonInformation class
and start querying it using the three methodologies demonstrated in the previous
sections. After creating a few documents containing different persons with different
roles, we can query for all persons with the role Administrator assigned to them.
The code is as follows:

```
await client.CreateDocumentAsync(
  collection.DocumentsLink,
  new PersonInformation
  {
    FirstName = "Riccardo",
    LastName = "Becker",
    DateOfBirth = new DateTime(1974, 12, 21),
    Roles = new List<Role>
    {
      new Role() { RoleName = "Administrator"},
      new Role() { RoleName = "User"},
      new Role() { RoleName = "Billing Administrator"}
    }
  }
);
await client.CreateDocumentAsync(
  collection.DocumentsLink,
  new PersonInformation
```

```
  {
    FirstName = "John",
    LastName = "Doe",
    DateOfBirth = new DateTime(1970, 1, 1),
    Roles = new List<Role>
    {
      new Role() { RoleName = "User"}
    }
  }
);
```

Using the WHERE clause

Using a WHERE clause inside the **Query Explorer** is straightforward. The following screenshot shows a query and the results of a query looking for users with the first name John:

Using a simple JOIN

In order to be able to retrieve all the users that have the role `Administrator`, we need to apply a `JOIN`. It is not comparable to RDBMS querying because we cannot simply use `select  * from c where c.Roles = "Administrator"`.

The following screenshot shows how to run a `JOIN` query inside the **Query Explorer** on the Azure portal, returning the results on the right-hand side:

This query selects from all users in the collection (their first name, last name, and all of their roles), but only those that have a `RoleName` equal to `User`. Replacing `User` with `Administrator` would result in only one document being returned since John Doe does not have this role.

Updating documents

After executing some basic SELECT queries against our collection, it is time to do some updating. This means looking up the document, changing information, and saving it to the collection. Consider the following C# code snippet:

Updating documents

In the following code snippets, we will update a document, set a new date of birth, and save the document to the collection.

> To enable faster processing, we store the DateTime fields as epoch values so that range queries are executed efficiently.

I used information from the official Azure blogs (http://azure.microsoft.com/blog/2014/11/19/working-with-dates-in-azure-documentdb-4/) to create the following code snippet. Instead of comparing dates, the corresponding epoch values are compared inside the query. First, a document is retrieved from the collection using a filter on the first and last name. A new date of birth value is created and written back to the collection. The code is as follows:

```
var documentByLinq = (from c in client
.CreateDocumentQuery<PersonInformation>(collection.DocumentsLink)
  where c.FirstName.Equals("Riccardo")
  && c.LastName.Equals("Becker")
  select c).AsEnumerable<PersonInformation>().First();

var newDoB = new DateEpoch
{
  Date = new DateTime(1974, 12, 22)
};

documentByLinq.DateOfBirth = newDoB;

ResourceResponse<Document> response = await
  client.ReplaceDocumentAsync(documentByLinq.SelfLink,
  documentByLinq);
//verify the update
var verifyUpdateLinq = (from c in client
.CreateDocumentQuery<PersonInformation>(collection.DocumentsLink)
```

```
where c.DateOfBirth.Epoch.Equals(newDoB.Epoch)
select c
).AsEnumerable<PersonInformation>().First();
Console.WriteLine(verifyUpdateLinq.FirstName + " " +
verifyUpdateLinq.LastName + " was born at " +
  verifyUpdateLinq.DateOfBirth.Date.ToShortDateString());
```

In **Document Explorer**, you can see that both the human-readable date of birth value and the epoch value is kept inside the document.

Deleting documents

In this section, we will demonstrate how to delete a document from your collection. DocumentDB does not support deleting batches of documents or a whole range of documents. You need to delete them one by one, using the SelfLink property.

The following code snippet demonstrates how to delete a single document:

```
var documentByLinqToObjects = client.CreateDocumentQuery<PersonInforma
tion>(collection.DocumentsLink)
  .Where(personInformation =>
    personInformation.FirstName.Equals("Riccardo")
  && personInformation.LastName.Equals(
    "Becker")).AsEnumerable<PersonInformation>().First();
  ////if the document exists, delete it and recreate it.
  if (null != documentByLinqToObjects)
  {
    await client.DeleteDocumentAsync(
      documentByLinqToObjects.SelfLink);
  }
```

Deleting a whole range of documents (if the query returns multiple documents) is not yet possible in one call. This is because we need the `SelfLink` property to the document in order to delete it. A possible workaround is to delete and recreate the collection if you want to delete all documents inside a collection. To delete a range of documents, you need to iterate through the result set and delete every single document by using the `SelfLink` property.

Summary

In this chapter, we saw how we can execute basic CRUD operations on our resources inside DocumentDB. We had a look at how to use SQL for DocumentDB, LINQ to objects, and plain LINQ. The importance of the `SelfLink` property was emphasized and we discussed how to enable your POCOs to contain this property. Next, we performed some basic querying operations by using simple WHERE clauses. Then, we demonstrated how to update resources and how to work with the specific `DateTime` fields by using epoch values. Finally, we saw how to delete documents from your collection.

In the next chapter, we will focus on more advanced querying techniques. We will also outline creating triggers, stored procedures, and user-defined functions.

4

Advanced Querying

This chapter will guide you through more advanced querying techniques. We will also focus on using built-in functions and creating triggers, stored procedures, and working with transactions. Finally, we will also create user-defined functions and demonstrate how to apply them in advanced queries.

Each section will discuss different querying techniques, showing both the DocumentDB SQL statements as well as the output.

In this chapter, we will cover the following topics:

* Learn about the SELECT, FROM, and WHERE statements in detail
* Learn how to apply operators in your queries
* Demonstrate how to use built-in functions
* Outline how to build stored procedures, triggers, and user-defined functions
* Discuss using LINQ to DocumentDB
* Learn how to work with transactions

At the time of writing, DocumentDB does not support aggregate functions like SUM or COUNT. Also, no GROUP BY is supported yet.

Using the SELECT statement

As we have seen in the previous chapters, the SELECT statement is the key to using DocumentDB and selecting, finding, and filtering resources inside your collections.

The SELECT statement is described in the following syntax convention:

```
<select_query> ::=
SELECT <select_specification>
    [ FROM <from_specification>]
    [ WHERE <filter_condition> ]
    [ ORDER BY <order_by_specification>]
```

As you can see, a SELECT statement consists of the SELECT keyword as well as (optionally) the FROM and WHERE clauses.

It is possible to execute only the SELECT statement, as we will see later in this chapter. The following code snippet shows a simple example of only a SELECT statement:

```
SELECT ABS(-1) returns
  [
    {
      "$1": 1
    }
  ]
```

Selecting some documents

In the previous chapters, we performed some basic querying against our collections. The following snippet is a simple query that returns all the first names inside the collection (the one we used in *Chapter 3, Basic Querying*).

Here's the query:

```
SELECT c.FirstName from c
```

Here's the output:

```
[
  {
    "FirstName": "Riccardo"
  },
  {
    "FirstName": "John"
  }
]
```

Using the FROM clause

The FROM clause is an optional clause, unless you want to apply filtering (by using the WHERE clause). The WHERE clause is used to specify the source(s) upon which the query needs to be executed. Mostly, the WHERE clause is used to select a collection. The FROM clause is needed when you want to query a collection.

Another example of using the SELECT statement without the FROM clause is the following code snippet:

```
SELECT CONTAINS(UPPER("Riccardo"), UPPER("ri"))
```

This SELECT statement only operates on string values and uses some of the built-in functions that DocumentDB provides (CONTAINS and UPPER). The output of this SELECT statement is as follows:

```
[
  {
    "$1": true
  }
]
```

Potentially, you could use DocumentDB only for its built-in functions, but it would be an expensive solution.

Aliasing

Collections can be aliased by applying the AS operator:

```
SELECT p.FirstName, p.LastName FROM PersonInformation AS p
```

Once we decide to use aliasing, we can no longeruse PersonInformation as the source. Consider the following code:

```
SELECT p.FirstName, PersonInformation.LastName FROM PersonInformation
AS p
```

The snippet fails since the identifier PersonInformation cannot be resolved since only the p alias is known.

Aliasing also means that all properties must be referenced by using the alias. Selecting FirstName from the aliased PersonInformation collection will fail because the property FirstName is no longer found due to the aliasing having been applied.

Joining documents

Since DocumentDB is schema-free, there is no such thing as joining tables like in the old RDBMS-world. Joining in a schema-free world is called a self-join.

Here's the query:

```
SELECT f.FirstName, f.LastName, c.RoleName
FROM Families f
JOIN c in f.Roles
WHERE c.RoleName="User"
```

Here's the output:

```
[
  {
    "FirstName": "Riccardo",
    "LastName": "Becker",
    "RoleName": "User"
  },
  {
    "FirstName": "John",
    "LastName": "Doe",
    "RoleName": "User"
  }
]
```

The preceding example shows a join between the document root and the subnode `Roles` and returns only those that have a role called `User`.

Selecting from subdocuments

A very interesting feature is to select from so-called subdocuments, enumerating only a subtree inside each document. In our case, all our documents (can) contain the `Roles` tree describing the user's roles. In my tests, I noticed that executing similar `SELECT` statements returning the exact same result set requires different numbers of RUs.

Here's the query:

```
select * from c.Roles f
select c.Roles from c
```

Here's the output:

```
[
  [
    {
      "RoleName": "Adminstrator"
    },
    {
      "RoleName": "User"
    },
    {
      "RoleName": "Billing Administrator"
    }
  ],
  [
    {
      "RoleName": "User"
    }
  ]
]
```

The number of RUs required for the first select is 2.4 and 2.45 for the second select. It is a minor difference but it can add up if you execute millions of SELECT statements.

> Please note that executing a SELECT statement against a subtree might require fewer RUs, so there is a cost factor involved. This is worth investigating if you architect your solution.

Using the WHERE clause

Filtering can be done by using the WHERE clause. The conditions we add in the clause will cause DocumentDB to filter the collection, and any document must evaluate the specified conditions to be true, otherwise they will not be part of the result set. To demonstrate several operators in the WHERE clause, our current PersonInformation document will be expanded with several properties. The support C# solution from *Chapter 3, Basic Querying*, will be upgraded with this new requirement:

- Every document will contain an indicator on how many devices this specific person has at home to support home automation
- An additional subtree containing the actual home automation devices including the price of the device will be added

This section will demonstrate multiple operators for the WHERE clause:

- Binary operators
- The BETWEEN keyword
- Logical operators
- The IN keyword
- Conditional expressions

Binary operators

Currently, DocumentDB supports the following binary operators:

Arithmetic	+, -, *, /, %
Bitwise	|, &, ^, <, >>, >>> (zero-fill right shift)
Logical	AND, OR, NOT
Comparison	=, ! =, <, >, <=, >=, <>
String	||

The BETWEEN keyword

Using the BETWEEN keyword can be very helpful for executing a query against a range of values. The following snippet shows how to get all persons who have at least one home automation device and at most three:

```
SELECT * FROM personInformation AS c
WHERE c.NumberOfHomeAutomationDevices BETWEEN 1 AND 3
```

Logical operators

Logical operators are applied to Boolean values or expressions. The following snippet shows the AND operator and, obviously, returns an empty result set:

```
SELECT * FROM personInformation p
where p.LastName = 'Becker' AND p.LastName='Doe'
```

Using the IN keyword

The IN keyword can be used to match a value within a list. The following snippet returns all documents where the LastName is Becker or Doe:

```
SELECT * FROM personInformation p
where p.LastName IN ('Becker', 'Doe')
```

Conditional expressions

The **ternary** and coalesce operators are the conditional expressions. The ternary operator (?) can be used to create new JSON properties when the query is executed. This is shown in the following code snippet:

```
SELECT (p.LastName = 'Becker') ? "The author" : "Some other person"
FROM personInformation p
```

The following snippet returns the string The author for every document that has the LastName property equal to Becker. Otherwise, it returns some other person.

The coalesce operator (??) can be used to check for the existence of a property inside a document. This can be useful when you have different types of documents inside the collection where new versions of documents appear. For example, the first version of your application does not contain the MiddleName property, but the second version of your application does. To write a query that supports both versions, we can use the ?? operator. The following snippet shows how to use it:

```
SELECT p.LastName, p.MiddleName ?? ",", p.FirstName   FROM
personInformation p
```

This query returns the LastName, MiddleName (only if the property exists, otherwise just a comma), and FirstName properties for all the documents inside the collection.

The coalesce operator can be very useful when you want to support different versions of your documents with a single query.

Using built-in functions

DocumentDB contains many built-in functions such as string manipulations, mathematical functions, type-checking functions or geospatial functions.

A simple description of how to use a built-in function is provided next:

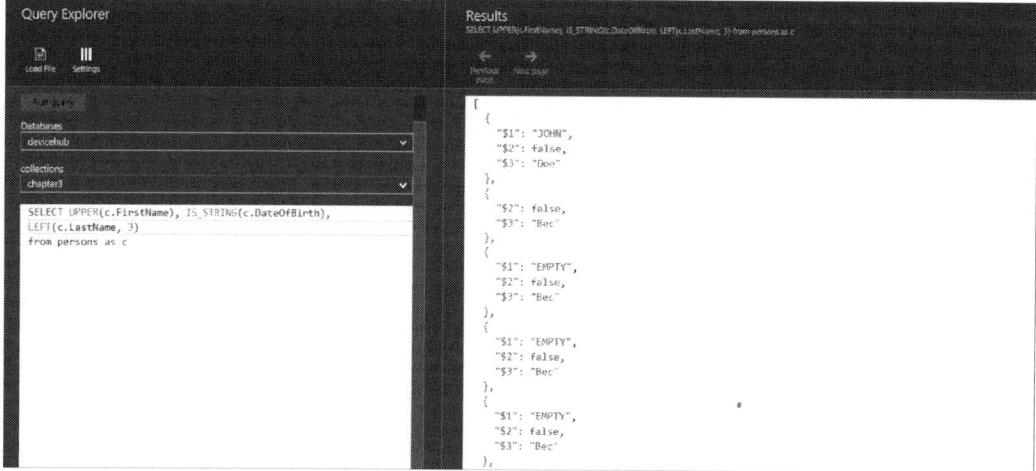

This sample script demonstrates the use of the built-in functions UPPER, IS_STRING, and LEFT.

Building stored procedures

Building a stored procedure is very straightforward. Stored procedures, triggers, and user-defined functions can be created by using the **Script Explorer** on the Azure portal:

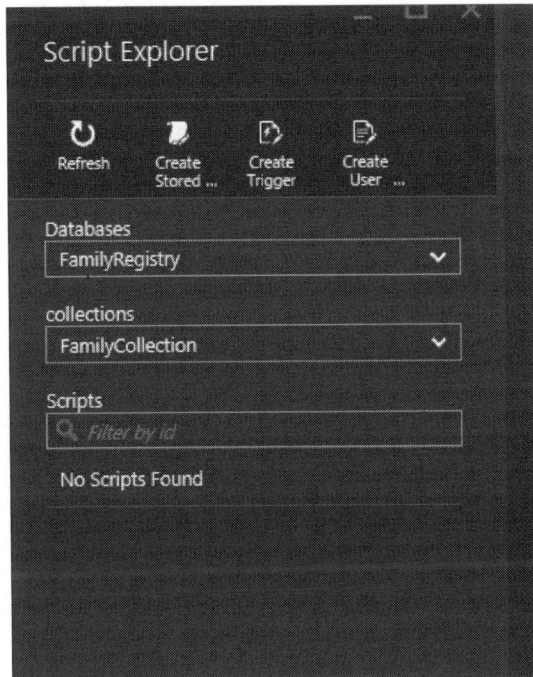

To create a new stored procedure, click on the **Create Stored Procedure** button.

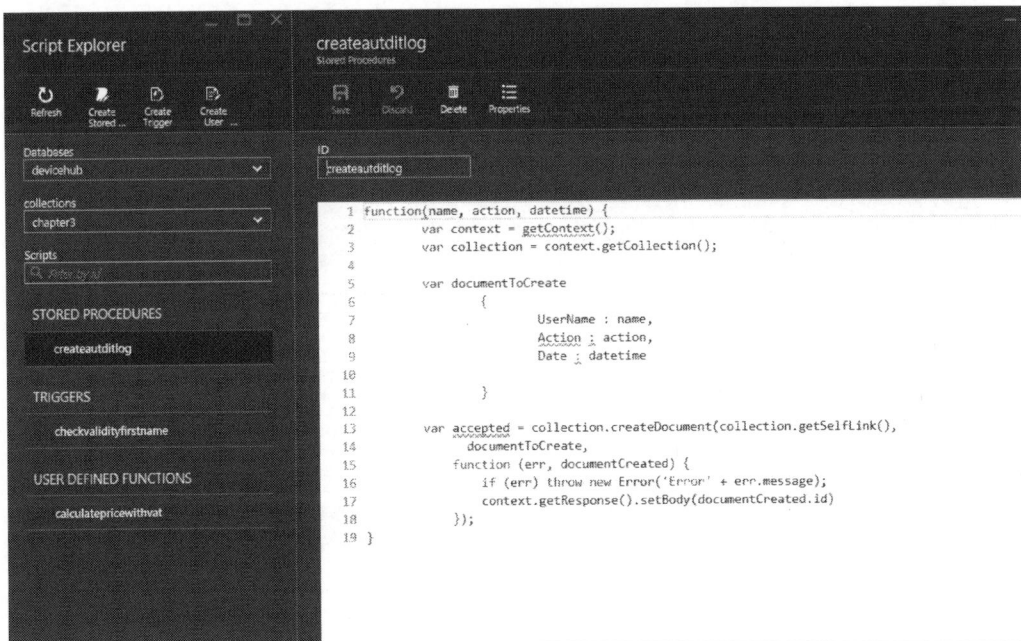

This stored procedure creates a separate document inside the collection containing the username, action, and date. This stored procedure can be used, for example, in the trigger we create later in this chapter to keep track of all the actions that are performed inside the system. At the time of writing, executing stored procedures from the **Query Explorer** in the Azure portal was not yet enabled.

> At the time of writing, executing stored procedures from the **Query Explorer** in the Azure portal is not possible.
>
> Try executing this stored procedure by using the code snippets that were provided in *Chapter 3, Basic Querying*.

Building triggers

A trigger is application logic or a business rule that is written in JavaScript. It looks similar to a function or method, but a trigger is only executed by the database engine when a document gets inserted, replaced, or deleted. Triggers can be useful, for example, to create an audit trail to keep track of all the changes in the system or to set default values for a document to be created.

The example trigger is a trigger that is fired before the actual insert (although triggers and their actual insert, replace, or delete actions on a document are inside one transaction) and checks for the first name. If it is not there or empty, it will set a default value. To test the trigger, we will also create a new property on the document affected.

The triggers get the property `FirstName` from the document involved (that is retrieved by `request.GetBody()`). If the property is not there or empty, it will set this `FirstName` property with the value `TheDefaultFirstName`. Additionally, a new property called `TestValue` is created. Finally, the body of the original request is replaced with the new document containing the changed and added properties.

The result of the trigger is shown in the following screenshot:

> Another **User-defined Function (UDF)** that is interesting is the `IS_DEFINED(param)` function. This function returns true if the `param` property exists on the document. Using this UDF can help you track missing properties or set default values for missing properties.

The next version of the trigger will contain a call to the `createauditlog` stored procedure.

Building user-defined functions

A UDF can be used to write custom business logic. UDFs can only be called from inside queries. A good example of a UDF inside our domain is produced by creating a function that calculates the price of a device including VAT.

UDFs can be created on the Azure portal, just like stored procedures and triggers. This UDF can be defined in the following way:

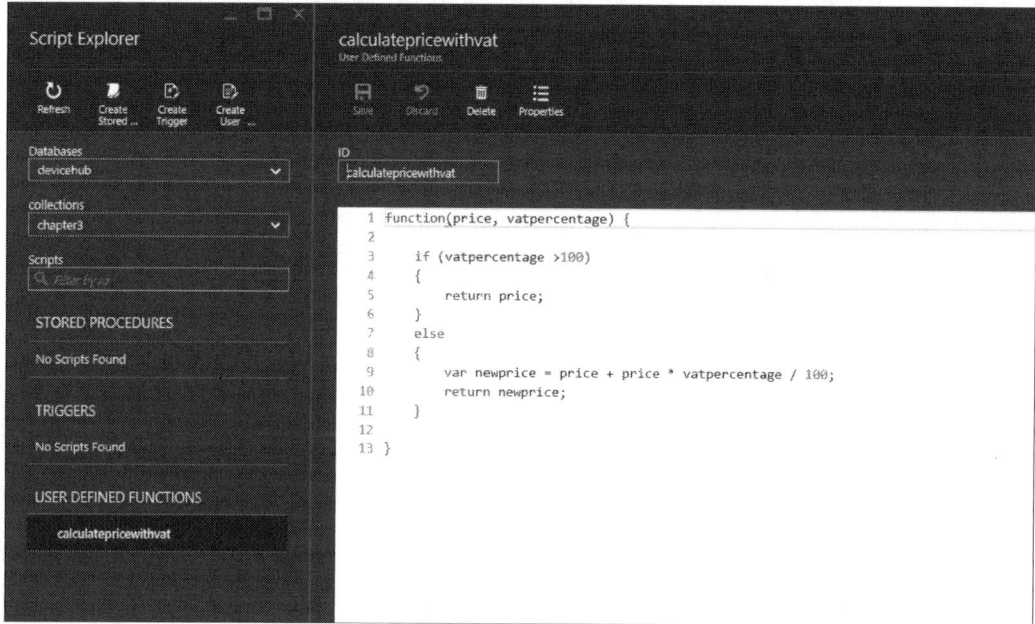

```
Script Explorer                    calculatepricewithvat
                                   User Defined Functions

  ↻        ▢        ▷        ▷       🖫        ↺        🗑        ☰
Refresh  Create   Create   Create   Save     Discard   Delete   Properties
         Stored...Trigger  User...

Databases                          ID
  devicehub                    ∨     calculatepricewithvat

collections                         1  function(price, vatpercentage) {
  chapter3                     ∨     2
                                     3      if (vatpercentage >100)
Scripts                              4      {
  🔍 Filter by id                     5          return price;
                                     6      }
STORED PROCEDURES                    7      else
                                     8      {
No Scripts Found                     9          var newprice = price + price * vatpercentage / 100;
                                    10          return newprice;
TRIGGERS                            11      }
                                    12
No Scripts Found                    13  }

USER DEFINED FUNCTIONS

    calculatepricewithvat
```

If the VAT exceeds 100 percent, the function just returns the price (the VAT is then probably invalid or a mistake). Otherwise, it returns the original price including VAT. Testing this UDF involves a simple query.

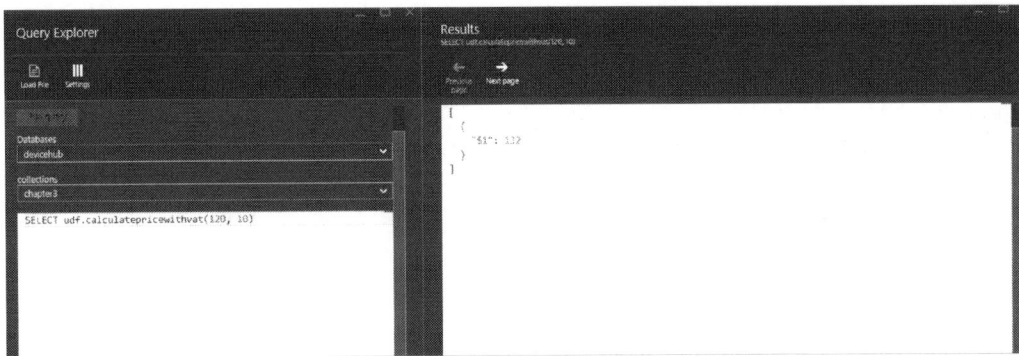

The UDF can also be included inside WHERE clauses of our queries.

Using LINQ to DocumentDB

We have already seen some aspects of LINQ to DocumentDB in previous chapters but in this section we describe it in much more detail. We have seen ways to query our database using SQL and JavaScript or directly on the portal.

Microsoft have also provided a .NET SDK for DocumentDB that includes a LINQ provider. LINQ is used by many developers and architects because it offers a programming model that is consistent across different underlying databases or stores. The a LINQ provider translates LINQ query to a DocumentDB query, reducing the complexity for the programmer. Instead of executing raw SQL queries against DocumentDB, we can create an IQueryable object that queries the DocumentDB query provider. The provider translates the LINQ query into an SQL query and executes it. The result set that contains the JSON is then deserialized into a .NET object on the client.

For example, the following LINQ statement is translated to DocumentDB SQL:

```
query.Where (p => p.LastName == "Becker")
```

In turn, this is translated by the provider to:

```
select * from personInformation p
where p.LastName = "Becker"
```

Summary

In this chapter, we discussed advanced querying options for our databases in great detail. First, we saw how to use the SELECT statement together with the FROM statement. We saw how to use JOIN operations and how to select from so-called subdocuments. Next, we discussed how to use the WHERE statement along with different operators such as BETWEEN, AND, and IN, and how to use conditional expressions.

In subsequent sections, we discussed how to use built-in functions. We saw how to write our own stored procedures, triggers, and user-defined functions. Finally, we talked about the LINQ provider for DocumentDB.

In the next chapter, you will learn about the REST protocol and how to use it to access DocumentDB resources. This will be demonstrated in C# snippets and by the use of an external tool called Fiddler.

5

Using REST to Access
Your Database

In this chapter, we will discuss how to operate against DocumentDB using the open REST protocol. There are different APIs and SDKs available for DocumentDB, such as .NET, Java, Python, Node.js, and JavaScript. For all other programming environments and platforms, there is the possibility to use the REST interface.

In this chapter, we will cover:

- The basics of the REST protocol
- How to use the REST API against DocumentDB
- Writing some C# code to support our demos
- Using the Fiddler tool to demonstrate the usage of the REST API

The Fiddler tool is free to download from `http://www.telerik.com/fiddler`.

Understanding the basics of REST

Representational State Transfer (REST) is a software architecture for building web services. REST communicates over HTTP using the HTTP verbs `GET`, `POST`, `PUT`, and `DELETE`. REST operations involve resources and the HTTP verbs indicate what actions to perform. The following sections describe the HTTP verbs in combination with REST and demonstrate some typical operations. The four above-mentioned verbs are sufficient to perform all the CRUD operations we need in modern systems.

Check out the following table to see the differences between the verbs and some examples:

Verb	Operation	Happy flow	Unhappy flow
POST	Creates a resource	POST/devices 201 created	404 not found or 409 conflict when item already exists
GET	Gets a resource	GET/devices Returns a list of all devices	GET/devices/{id} Returns a specific device or 404 not found if the device does not exist
PUT	Updates a resource	PUT/devices Potentially updates the complete collections of devices	PUT/devices/{id} Updates the specific device or returns a 404 not found if the device does not exist.
DELETE	Deletes a resource	DELETE/devices Deletes the complete collection of devices. For data safety reasons, this operation should be carefully implemented.	DELETE/devices/{id} Returns a 200 if successful or a 404 not found if the device ID cannot be found in the devices collection

A web service can be labeled as RESTful if it conforms to several constraints described in the following table:

Constraint	Description
Client-server	This involves a strict separation of concerns. Clients are not concerned about persisting data, which is the full responsibility of the server. On the other hand, servers are not concerned about the calling party or what technology is used on the client side. Since servers are not strictly bound to their clients, REST servers can be simple and very scalable (since there is no state). The most important aspect in this constraint is that the interface between clients and servers remains the same, while the underlying technology can change at any time.
Stateless	The server maintains no state between different requests. Every single request from a client should contain all the information that is needed to be able to properly service the request. The server can persist the state, for example, in a database (or a DocumentDB collection).

Constraint	Description
Cacheable	Server responses can be cacheable if applicable. This is most appropriate for the GET request, since caching a POST request on the client does not really make sense. Proper caching can eliminate the traffic between clients and the server which increases performance.
Uniform interface	An important aspect of REST is the uniform interface that simplifies and decouples the REST architecture. This allows systems to change and evolve independently.

Using the GET verb

The HTTP GET method is used to retrieve a resource or a list of resources. The GET verb returns XML or JSON format data and a HTTP response 200 (OK). When the GET fails for some reason it returns response codes in the 400 range like 404 NOT FOUND or 400 Bad Request.

As the GET verb implies, it should be used only for reading data and not manipulating it. Although it is possible to build REST services using the GET verb to modify data, it is bad practice.

The GET verb is idempotent since it does not change the data.

Using the POST verb

The POST verb is intended to be used for creating a new resource. If the POST is successful, it should return the HTTP status 201.

The POST verb is not idempotent, since calling the POST method multiple times will result in multiple resources being created (unless the underlying business logic prevents this).

Using the PUT verb

The PUT verb should be used to update resources. A PUT request contains a body with the new state of a resource (not only updated fields example) that replaces the original resource.

A successful PUT request returns a 200. Sometimes, PUT can be used to create resources (instead of POST) if the client is responsible for choosing a unique identifier. In this case, the PUT request contains a unique identifier that does not exist on the server side yet. This practice is possible, though not very common, and should be used carefully. The PUT verb is idempotent, since changing the state of a resource multiple times with the same message body only changes the original resource once.

Using the DELETE verb

The DELETE verb is used to delete a resource or a range of resources.

The DELETE verb is idempotent, since deleting a resource multiple times does not affect the state. The resource is gone and remains deleted. It is good practice to return a 404 when you try to delete a resource multiple times, since the resource does not exist anymore.

Querying DocumentDB resources

This section covers how to use REST to query DocumentDB resources. Each resource has a corresponding URI. The database account is managed by the Azure Management API and the base URI for a DocumentDB is `https://management.azure.com/subscriptions/{subscriptionid}/resourcegroups/{resourcegroupname}/providers/Microsoft.DocumentDB/databaseAccounts/{accountname}`.

- The `subscriptionid` is the Azure subscription that is the owner of the database
- The `resourcegroupname` is the resource group that the account is under
- The `accountname` is the database account name

The base URI for the rest of the resources are based on the URI endpoint that is specifically created for the database account name. The following table shows the base URI for each type of resource:

Resources	Base URI
Database	`https://{databaseaccount}.documents.azure.com/dbs/{_rid-db}`
User	`https://{databaseaccount}.documents.azure.com/dbs/{_rid-db}/users/{_rid-user}`
Permission	`https://{databaseaccount}.documents.azure.com/dbs/{_rid-db}/users/{_rid-user}/permissions/{_rid-perm}`
Collection	`https://{databaseaccount}.documents.azure.com/dbs/{_rid-db}/colls/{_rid-coll}`
Stored procedure	`https://{databaseaccount}.documents.azure.com/dbs/{_rid-db}/colls/{_rid-coll}/sprocs/{_rid-sproc}`

Resources	Base URI
Trigger	`https://{databaseaccount}.documents.azure.com/dbs/{_rid-db}/colls/{_rid-coll}/triggers/{_rid-trigger}`
UDF	`https://{databaseaccount}.documents.azure.com/dbs/{_rid-db}/colls/{_rid-coll}/udfs/{_rid-udf}`
Document	`https://{databaseaccount}.documents.azure.com/dbs/{_rid-db}/colls/{_rid-coll}/docs/{_rid-doc}`
Attachment	`https://{databaseaccount}.documents.azure.com/dbs/{_rid-db}/colls/{_rid-coll}/docs/{_rid-doc/attachments/{_rid-attch}`

Setting request headers

In order to be able to perform query operations against DocumentDB, the following headers need to be set:

Standard header	Description
`Authorization`	The authentication type and signature token. This is required. Only the master key token is allowed for this operation.
`Content-Type`	This is optional. Must be set to `application/query+json`.

This table can be found at `https://msdn.microsoft.com/en-us/library/dn783363.aspx`.

> The `Content-Type` does not seem to be required, although it is specified in any case.

Generating the authorization header

Before we can use REST to operate against our DocumentDB, we need to generate the right authorization header for every request. The following C# snippets are used to do so:

```
/// <summary>
/// This method creates a signature based on masterkey,
    resourceId (if any), resourcetype
/// verb (default = GET) and dates (if any)
/// </summary>
/// <param name="masterKey">MasterKey of DocumentDB
    database</param>
```

```csharp
/// <param name="resourceId">_rid of the resource involved (if
  any)</param>
/// <param name="resourceType">docs or colls etc.</param>
/// <param name="verb">GET, POST etc.</param>
/// <returns></returns>
public static string GetSignature(string masterKey, string
  resourceId, string resourceType, string verb = "GET")
{
  const string AuthorizationFormat = "type={0}&ver={1}&sig={2}";
  const string MasterToken = "master";
  const string TokenVersion = "1.0";

  //always use datetime.UtcNow
  var xDate = DateTime.UtcNow.ToString("r");

  var masterKeyBytes = Convert.FromBase64String(masterKey);
  var hmacSha256 = new HMACSHA256(masterKeyBytes);
  var resourceIdInput = resourceId ?? string.Empty;
  var resourceTypeInput = resourceType ?? string.Empty;

  var payLoad = string.Format(CultureInfo.InvariantCulture,
    "{0}\n{1}\n{2}\n{3}\n{4}\n",
    verb.ToLowerInvariant(),
    resourceTypeInput.ToLowerInvariant(),
    resourceIdInput.ToLowerInvariant(),
    (xDate ?? string.Empty).ToLowerInvariant(),
    String.Empty);
  //compute the hash of this payload
  var hashPayLoad = hmacSha256.ComputeHash(
    Encoding.UTF8.GetBytes(payLoad));
  //generate token
  var authorizationToken = Convert.ToBase64String(hashPayLoad);

  //encode and return the token
  return System.Web.HttpUtility.UrlEncode(string.Format(
    CultureInfo.InvariantCulture,
    AuthorizationFormat,
    MasterToken,
    TokenVersion,
    authorizationToken));
}
```

Depending on the verb (GET, POST, and so on), the resourceType (dbs, colls, or docs), the resourceId (optional), and the master key that can be found in the Azure portal, the authorization key is generated.

Getting all databases

In order to get a list of all the databases inside a collection, we use the following C# snippet:

```
client.DefaultRequestHeaders.Add("x-ms-date", DateTime.UtcNow.
ToString("r"));
client.DefaultRequestHeaders.Add("x-ms-version", "2015-08-06");
//get signature based on masterkey and the resourcetype dbs (no
    resourceId involved yet).
signature = GetSignature(masterKey, "", "dbs", "GET");
client.DefaultRequestHeaders.Add("authorization", signature);
string getResponse = client.GetStringAsync(new Uri(baseUri,
    "dbs")).Result;
```

Using Fiddler to enter the raw REST input, we get the following result:

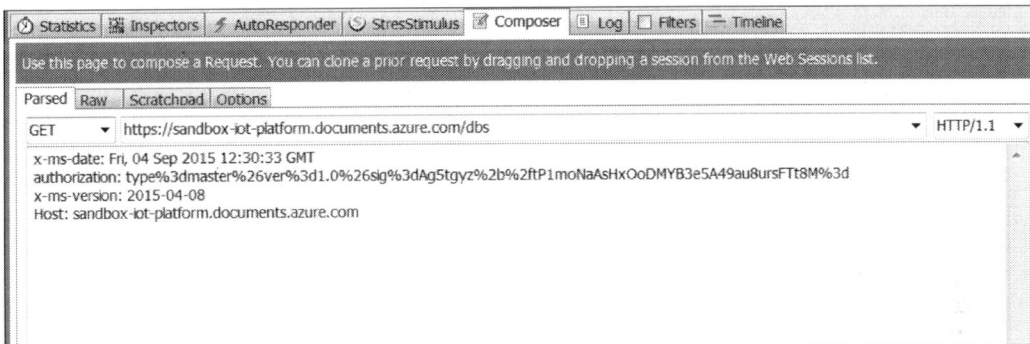

The output of this REST call is shown in the following screenshot:

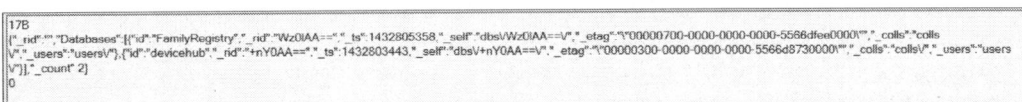

Adding a document

The following snippets show how to create a document in a certain collection:

```
//get signature based on masterkey, collection resource id and
resource type documents (docs)
signature = GetSignature(masterKey, collectionRid, "docs", "POST");
client.DefaultRequestHeaders.Remove("authorization");
```

```
client.DefaultRequestHeaders.Add("authorization", signature);

string json = JsonConvert.SerializeObject(new
{
  id = Guid.NewGuid().ToString(),
  test = "hello DocumentDB, created via REST API!"
});
HttpContent contentPost = new StringContent(json);
//add payload to body
//do the post against the REST API and create the document
var postResponse = client.PostAsync(new Uri(baseUri,
  string.Format("dbs/{0}/colls/{1}/docs",
  deviceHubDb.ResourceId, collectionRid)),
contentPost).Result;
Console.WriteLine(postResponse.ReasonPhrase);
```

This time, we need to use the POST verb (which affects the authorization key as well). The payload of the PostAsync call is a JSON file and the final status code is created.

Again, the REST representation of this operation in Fiddler is shown in the following screenshot:

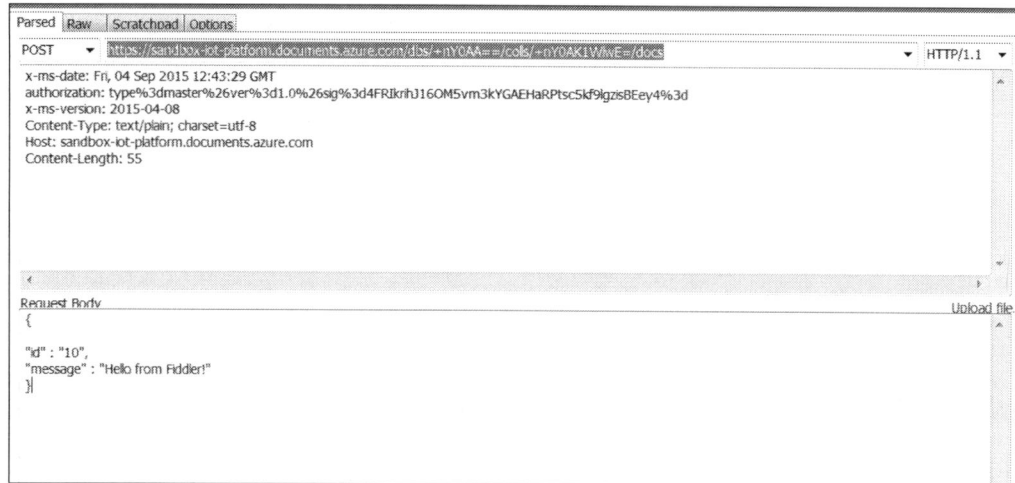

Now that we have seen how to use the GET and POST verb against the REST API of DocumentDB, we can execute all operations needed in an enterprise scenario for platforms that do not have a DocumentDB SDK available.

The source projects also demonstrate how to get the right collection (similar to listing all databases) by providing a resource ID representing the designated database.

Summary

In this chapter, we covered the very basics of the REST protocol and what verbs are available in the protocol. We saw that every single resource inside our DocumentDB can be referenced by a unique URI. This URI is the basis for executing REST-based queries against our databases, collections, documents, and all other available resources. We wrote some C# code in order to generate the authorization key that is needed for every REST request. Finally, we fired some REST queries against our DocumentDB to get a list of all the databases and how to create a document inside a collection. We used C# and we saw the raw HTTP representations of the same queries inside Fiddler.

In the next chapter, you will learn how to use Node.js to perform a subset of the activities from this chapter. The focus will be on how to use DocumentDB from Node.js to kick-start your Node.js projects.

6

Using Node.js to Access Your Database

In this chapter, we'll see how to operate against DocumentDB using Node.js. There are different APIs and SDKs available for DocumentDB, such as .NET, Java, Python, Node.js, and JavaScript. For all other programming environments and platforms, there is the possibility to use the REST interface.

In this chapter, we will cover the following:

- Learn how to setup your development environment for Node.js
- Perform some basic operations against DocumentDB using Node.js
- Deploy a Node.js application to Microsoft Azure and test it

Introducing Node.js

Node.js is gaining a lot of popularity during the last years and more and more developers embrace Node.js. But what is it and why should we use it?

What is Node.js?

Node.js is a runtime system for creating server applications. The core of Node.js is a bare, stripped server that accepts requests and can respond to them. All this occurs in a so called *loop*. There is no underlying *web server* like Internet Information Server or Apache needed to run Node.js. Every request to a Node.js application spins off a new thread on the server. This means that the main thread in Node.js never gets blocked and that potentially it can serve thousands and thousands of concurrent users. On http://nodejs.org, you can find lots of information and examples of Node.js.

The most basic example of a Node.js application is shown here:

```
var http = require('http');
http.createServer(function (req, res) {
  res.writeHead(200, {'Content-Type': 'text/plain'});
  res.end('Hello World\n');
}).listen(1337, "127.0.0.1");
```

This snippet creates a server and starts listening for requests on port 1337. Every request is replied to with Hello World.

Why use Node.js?

Node.js is built and designed for performance and scalability. It is also a great candidate to build RESTful APIs, since it can handle thousands of concurrent requests. Since Node.js is a JavaScript runtime built on Chrome's V8 JavaScript engine, developers with JavaScript knowledge can easily start using Node.js without having a steep learning curve. Another advantage is that Node.js can run on any platform and in our case, we can easily deploy and start it on the Microsoft Azure platform.

Preparing Visual Studio 2015

In order to turn Visual Studio 2015 into a suitable development environment for Node.js, we need to install the Node.js tools for Visual Studio. These tools can be downloaded from https://www.visualstudio.com/en-us/features/node-js-vs.aspx. Installing these tools will add:

- Project templates to enable an easy start for developing Node.js apps.

- IntelliSense to all Node.js code.

- NPM integration. **Node Package Manager (NPM)** gets installed with the Node.js tools. The NPM enables you to pull Node.js packages to your solution. At some level, it is comparable to the NuGet package manager.

- Enable Node.js code in an interactive window.

- Profiling and debugging capabilities.

For more information on Node.js, please visit https://nodejs.org/en/.

Building our first Node.js application

In this section, we'll start building our first Node.js application with Visual Studio. We'll also get to know more about the tools we just installed. Finally, we'll publish our application to Microsoft Azure and bring our tool online.

Creating our first app

In Visual Studio, start a new project and select the installed template **Basic Azure Node.js Express 4 Application**.

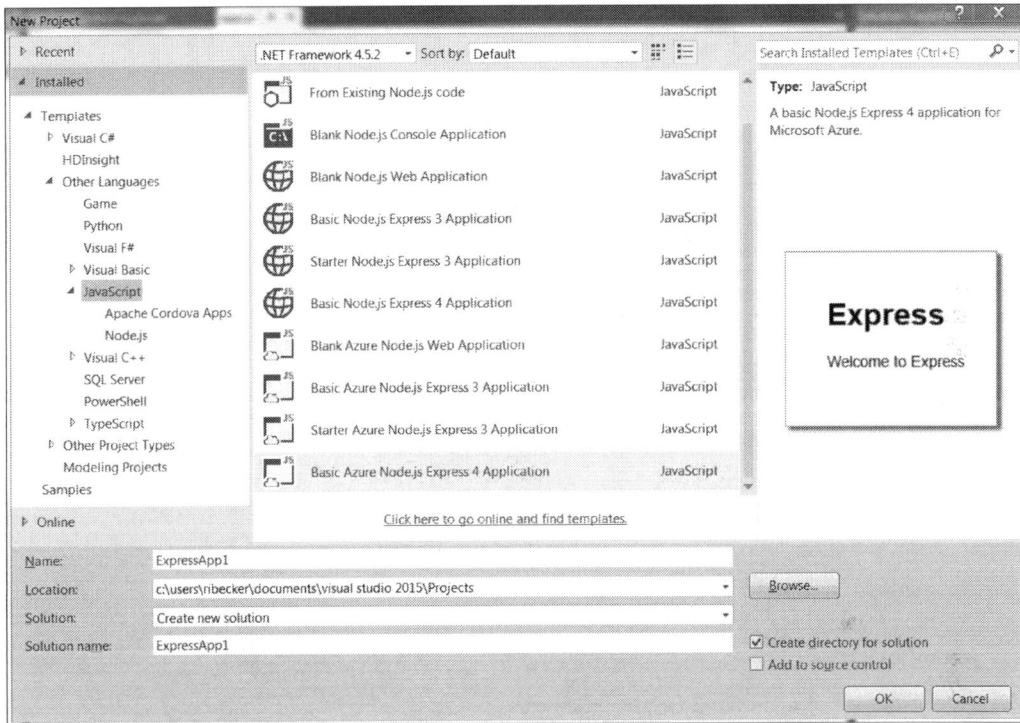

Selecting this template and clicking on the **OK** button will give you a fresh Node.js project that can already be started locally on our own machine.

Creating a web app

Publishing the application we have just created to Microsoft Azure and making it available for the whole world requires some steps.

To start the publishing process, right-click on the Node.js project we have just created. Select the **Publish** option and the following dialogue appears:

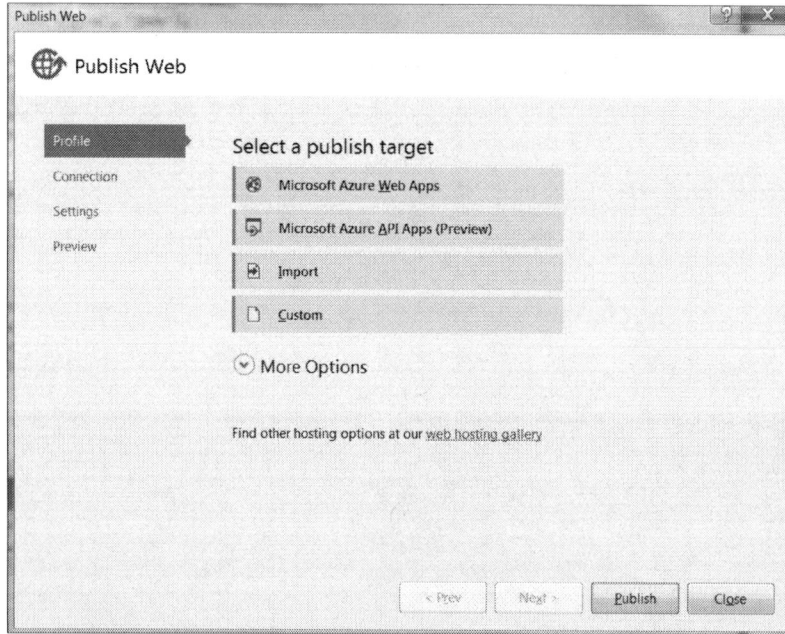

Select the option **Microsoft Azure Web Apps**. Enter the login credentials for your Azure subscription (if not logged in already) and select the **New...** button.

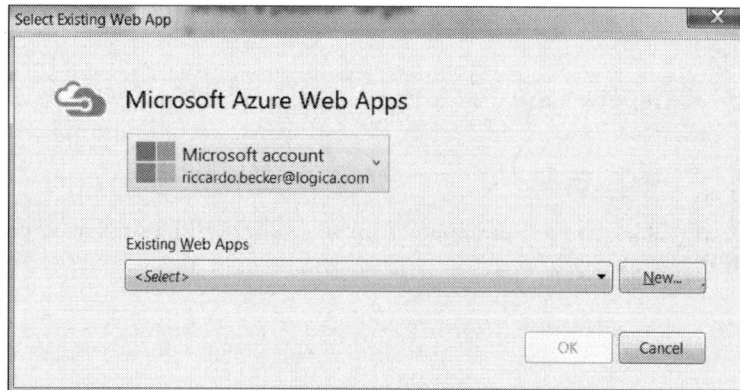

Enter a unique name for the web application and enter valid values for **App Service plan**, **Resource group**, and **Region**. Then, click on **Create**. Your Node.js web application will be created and published.

When the publishing process is successful, your Node.js application can be accessed on `http://<WEBAPPNAME>.azurewebsites.net/`.

Using Visual Studio 2015 and the Node.js tools, we were able to create and publish our first Node.js application in less than five minutes. The next sections will focus on using DocumentDB from our Node.js application.

Utilizing DocumentDB from Node.js

This section will cover how to build a Node.js application that is using the DocumentDB basics we discussed in the previous chapters. In this section, we will cover:

- Preparing our Node.js project
- Connecting to our DocumentDB account
- Querying documents using Node.js
- Creating a document using Node.js

Preparing our project

To use DocumentDB from our existing example project, we need to install some modules. Modules are maintained in the `package.json` file inside our project. Installing additional modules will modify this JSON file with new entries. When deploying our new functionality to Azure, this file is used to determine what additional modules need to be installed on our Azure node.

We can install additional modules using the Node.js interactive window. This window can be activated from the **View** menu of Visuals Studio or by using the shortcut keys *Ctrl + K, N*. We need to install two additional modules called `async` and `documentdb`.

```
Node.js Interactive Window
  .help                    Show a list of REPL commands
  .clear                   Resets the context object to an empty object and clears any multi-line expression.
  .cls                     Clears the contents of the REPL editor window
  .echo                    Suppress or unsuppress output to the buffer
  .npm                     Executes npm command. If solution contains multiple projects, specify target project using .npm [ProjectName]
<npm arguments>
  .reset                   Reset to an empty execution engine, but keep REPL history
  .save                    Save the current REPL session to a file
  .wait                    Wait for at least the specified number of milliseconds
> .npm install async --save
async@1.4.2 node_modules\async
install async --save successfully completed
> .npm install documentdb --save
npm WARN package.json async@1.4.2 No README data
documentdb@1.2.2 node_modules\documentdb
install documentdb --save successfully completed
>
```

Our project is now ready to use the DocumentDB libraries for Node.js.

The module `documentdb` contains methods for creating database, collection and documents equivalent to the DocumentDB .NET SDK and the REST API.

Connecting to DocumentDB

To connect to a DocumentDB account, we need some information like hostname, keys, database, and collection.

Create a new file called `configuration.js` and enter the following code snippet:

```
var config = {}

config.host = "<URI TO YOUR DOCUMENTDB ACCOUNT>";
config.authKey = "<YOURKEY>";
config.databaseId = "<YOUR DATABASE>";
config.collectionId = "<YOUR COLLECTION>";

module.exports = config;
```

This configuration file will be used to create a DocumentDB client in Node.js.

We will demonstrate the use inside the already created `index.js`. Add the following statements to the top of `index.js`:

```
var DocumentDBClient = require('documentdb').DocumentClient;
var config = require('../configuration');
```

These statements will include the module `documentdb` that we have installed in our project and it will enable the use of the configuration module we have just created.

With these snippets in place, we are able to connect to our DocumentDB environment.

```
var client = new DocumentDBClient(config.host,
  { masterKey: config.authKey });
```

The host and the `authKey` are taken from the configuration module. The `client` variable will be passed to the utilities module we will create in the next section.

Creating a module

Before we start operating against our database with Node.js, we need to create a utility module called `utils.js`. Copy the following snippet to `utils.js`:

```
//we require the DocumentDB node.js package
var DocumentDBClient = require('documentdb').DocumentClient;

//creat utils class that exposes functionality
var utils = {
  //go find a database
  getOrCreateDatabase: function (client, databaseId, callback) {
  var querySpec = {
  query: 'SELECT * FROM root r WHERE r.id=@id',
  parameters: [{
  name: '@id',
  value: databaseId
  }]
};
//search for our DB
client.queryDatabases(querySpec).toArray(function (err, results) {
if (err) {
  callback(err);
```

```
    } else {
    if (results.length === 0) {
      var databaseSpec = {
      id: databaseId
    };
    //no db, that's why we create one
    client.createDatabase(databaseSpec, function (err, created) {
    callback(null, created);
});

    } else {
      //db already exists, return it
      callback(null, results[0]);
      }
    }
});
    },

    //get or create a collection inside the db
    getOrCreateCollection: function (client, databaseLink, collectionId,
    callback) {
    var querySpec = {
      query: 'SELECT * FROM root r WHERE r.id=@id',
      parameters: [{
      name: '@id',
      value: collectionId
      }]
    };

    client.queryCollections(databaseLink, querySpec).toArray(function
    (err, results) {
      if (err) {
        callback(err);

    } else {
      if (results.length === 0) {
        var collectionSpec = {
        id: collectionId
      };

      var requestOptions = {
        offerType: 'S1'
      };
```

```
    //create a S1 collection inside the database and return
    client.createCollection(databaseLink, collectionSpec,
requestOptions, function (err, created) {
    callback(null, created);
    });

    } else {
    //return database
    callback(null, results[0]);
    }
    }
    });
},

    find: function (client, collection, querySpec, callback) {
    var self = this;

    client.queryDocuments(collection._self, querySpec).toArray(function
(err, results) {
    if (err) {
    callback(err);

    } else {
    callback(null, results);
    }
    });
    },

    //create a dummy document containing two properties
    createDocument : function (client, collection, callback) {
    var document = {
    FirstName : "Jane",
    LastName : "Doe"
    }
    client.createDocument(collection._self, document, function (err,
doc) {
    if (err) {
    //something went wrong, return the error
    callback(err);

    } else {
    //success, return the document
    callback(null, doc);
    }
```

```
      });
  }
};

  module.exports = utils;
```

This module contains a few helper functions:

- `getOrCreateDatabase(client, databaseId)` returns or creates the database based on the DocumentDB client and the `databaseId`, which is the logical name

- `getOrCreateCollection(client, databaseLink, collectionId)` returns or creates a collection based on the DocumentDB client, the link of the database, and the logical name of the collection

- `find(client, collection, querySpec)` queries the collection with the query specified in `querySpec` and returns all documents that match the query

- `createDocument` creates a constant document where `FirstName` is `Jane` and `LastName` is `Doe`

Now that we have our utilities in place, we can start creating a document and afterwards find that same document. The result will be displayed in the index view which is standard part of our solution.

Creating and finding a document

Add the following code snippet to `index.js`:

```
var DocumentDBClient = require('documentdb').DocumentClient;

//create documentDB client using the hostname and masterkey
var client = new DocumentDBClient(config.host,
  { masterKey: config.authKey });

var database, collection, results;
var docCreatedMessage;
var docFoundMessage;

//try get or else create the database and callback to
createDatabaseCallback
utils.getOrCreateDatabase(client, config.databaseId,
createDatabaseCallback);
```

```
function createDatabaseCallback(err, db) {
  if (err) {
    console.warn('error');
  } else {
  if (db) { //try get or create the collection and callback to
createCollectionCallBack
  utils.getOrCreateCollection(client, db._self, config.collectionId,
createCollectionCallBack);
  }
}
};

function createCollectionCallBack(err, coll)
{
  if (err) {

  } else {
  if (coll) { //try creating a document and callback to
createDocumentCallBack
  utils.createDocument(client, coll, createDocumentCallBack);
  }
}
}

//
function createDocumentCallBack(err, result) {
  if (err) {

  } else {
  //creating document was succesful, now run a SQL statement using
WHERE clause and callback to
  //findDocumentCallback
  utils.find(client, collection, "select * from entities r where
r.FirstName='Jane'", findDocumentCallBack);
  }
}

function findDocumentCallBack(err, result) {
  if (err) {

  } else {
  results = result[0]; //only the first document to demonstrate
```

```
docFoundMessage = "Yes we found a document matching our query :" +
results.FirstName + " " + results.LastName + "!";
docCreatedMessage = "Document created succesfully!";
//pass the found information back to the index view
router.get('/', function (req, res) {
res.render('index', {
title: 'Chapter 6!',
document: docCreatedMessage + "\n" + docFoundMessage
});
});
}
}
```

```
module.exports = router;
```

This snippet processes in an asynchronous way (this is what Node.js is all about) the following steps:

1. Get a reference to our database.
2. Get a reference to the collection.
3. Create a document.
4. Find the document based on a WHERE clause.

When all asynchronous operations are successfully executed, the index view is displayed inside your browser and shows the results of our snippet. To make the code easy to read, we have used callback functions.

Chapter 6!

Welcome to Chapter 6!

Document= Document created succesfully! Yes we found a document matching our query :Jane Doe!

Summary

In this chapter we discussed how to set up Visual Studio 2015 to start using Node.js in an integrated way. We have installed Node.js packages using the NPM with the Node.js interactive window. Next, we connected to our DocumentDB and we saw how to create a separate module that contains our DocumentDB credentials. Before operating against our database, we created a utility class that contains some helper functions. Finally, we used the utilities module to connect to our database, find the appropriate collection, create a document, search for that document, and display the successful results in the browser window.

In the next chapter, we will cover how to use indexes and how to modify them. We will also discuss the use of partitioning in case we need to scale out our collections. Next, we will have a look at how to measure performance, learn about transactions, and discuss consistency levels in detail.

7
Advanced Techniques

This chapter describes advanced techniques for the management of DocumentDB. We can use these techniques to optimize the way our documents are queried. When our application and data grows, we need to partition our data and spread it across multiple collections. When traffic increases, measuring performance is necessary to identify bottlenecks in our DocumentDB architecture.

In this chapter, we will:

- Learn about indexes and how to use them effectively
- Have a look at partitions and partitioning techniques
- Measure performance
- Learn about transactions
- See how consistency levels can be set and how they affect DocumentDB

Introducing indexes

As we discussed before, DocumentDB is a schema-free database containing JSON documents. By default, DocumentDB applies indexing to all document properties. This means you can specifically query for all the properties inside a document.

Explaining default indexing

Internally, DocumentDB represents all documents as trees. A dummy root node is created to make every document accessible via this root node. Every property of a document is a node in the tree representation.

The following code illustrates how one of our `PersonInformation` class's document is represented as a tree in JSON:

```
{
  "LastName": "Doe",
  "FirstName": "John",
  "DateOfBirth": {
    "Date": "1971-01-01T00:00:00",
    "Epoch": 31536000
  },
  "NumberOfHomeAutomationDevices": 1,
  "HomeAutomationDevices": [
    {
      "Manufacturer": "Contoso Inc.",
      "Type": "Heater",
      "Location": "Attic",
      "Price": 50
    }
  ],
  "Roles": [
    {
      "RoleName": "User"
    }
  ]
}
```

Here's the tree representation:

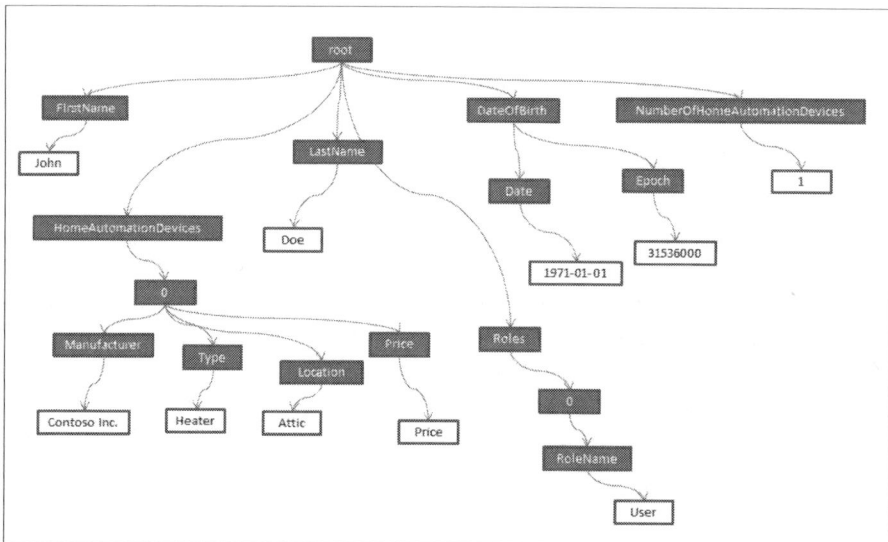

The actual values of the document are represented by the white squares containing the value.

> To be able to represent a document as a tree, a root node is added since documents do not contain root nodes by default (although you could create one).

By default, every path in a tree is indexed. We can override this indexing.

Customizing indexing policies

For a lot of scenarios, sticking to the default indexing that DocumentDB will suffice. DocumentDB also supports specifying an indexing policy for collections. This is done during the creating of the collection. Creating indexing policies enables you to choose between performance, consistency, and storage overhead.

The following concepts can be modified by using indexing policies:

- **Configuring index update mode**: This can be **Consistent, Lazy**, or **None**. We will explain these later in this section
- **Including or excluding documents and paths from indexing**: We can choose to exclude entire documents or paths inside the document from being indexed
- **Specifying the index type**: When configuring indexing on paths inside documents, we can specify the type of index and the precision for these paths

Configuring index update mode

DocumentDB offers three indexing modes that we can choose from. This indexing mode is configured using an indexing policy on a collection.

Consistent indexing mode

When a collection is configured with the **Consistent** mode, all inserts and/or updates to the collection are handled synchronously with the update to the index (if any). This mode comes with a cost because it reduces the write throughput. Besides writing the changes to the document to the database, it also needs to update the indexes immediately. This mode is useful if you want to make sure that every update to a document (which affects an index) is immediately reflected back to the collection. Users and applications can immediately query using those new indexes.

Lazy indexing mode

The **Lazy** indexing mode offers the highest document throughput. The changed indexes for the affected documents and properties are updated "later" and this moment is undeterministic. This means that when the throughput capacity is not fully used, the indexes are updated asynchronously. This mode can be useful when you insert a lot of documents during nightly batches, for example. Following a large number of writes during the night and after the batch uploads, the indexes get updated. In the morning, all documents are inserted and indexed so that applications and users can effectively query the documents again.

Setting the indexing mode to `Lazy` also reduces the number of request units needed for a batch upload of documents because no indexing needs to be done.

> Please note that setting the indexing mode to None can only be done when automatic indexing is turned off explicitly for the collection involved.

None indexing mode

Selecting the **None** indexing mode results in a collection with no indexes at all. This can be useful if you use DocumentDB for storage purposes only. You can still query documents by using the `id` and the `selflink` properties.

> Please note that setting the indexing mode to None can only be done when automatic indexing is turned off explicitly for the collection involved.

The following code snippets will set the different indexing modes and turn off automatic indexing:

```
var collection = new DocumentCollection { Id = "chapter7" };

//choose any of these three indexing modes
//collection.IndexingPolicy.IndexingMode = IndexingMode.Consistent;
//collection.IndexingPolicy.IndexingMode = IndexingMode.Lazy;
collection.IndexingPolicy.IndexingMode = IndexingMode.None;

//comment the next line if you want to use other IndexMode.
Consistent or IndexMode.Lazy
  collection.IndexingPolicy.Automatic = false;

  collection = await client.CreateDocumentCollectionAsync(database.
SelfLink, collection);
```

After successful creation of the `chapter7` collection, setting the `IndexingMode` to `None`, and setting the `IndexPolicy.Automatic` to `false`, you will get an exception if you decide to query this collection.

The following code snippet tries to query the `chapter7` collection but an exception is raised:

```
DocumentCollection collection = client.CreateDocumentCollectionQuery((
String)database.SelfLink).
  ToList().Where(cl => cl.Id.Equals("chapter7")).FirstOrDefault();

  //does this throw an exception?
  try
  {
    var documentByLinq = (from c in client.CreateDocumentQuery<PersonI
nformation>(collection.DocumentsLink)
    where c.FirstName.Equals("Riccardo")
    && c.LastName.Equals("Becker")
    select c).AsEnumerable<PersonInformation>().FirstOrDefault();
  }
  catch (Exception ex)
  {
    Console.WriteLine(ex.Message);
  }
```

The following exception is raised:

```
{"Errors":["A query has been specified for a document collection
with indexing mode 'none'. Consider adding allow scan header in the
request."]}
```

There is still a way to query non-indexed collections by using the `EnableScanInQuery` property of the `FeedOptions` class and pass it to the `CreateDocumentQuery` call. The code is as follows:

```
FeedOptions options = new FeedOptions();
options.EnableScanInQuery = true;

var documentByLinq = (from c in client.CreateDocumentQuery<PersonInfor
mation>(collection.DocumentsLink, options)
  where c.FirstName.Equals("Riccardo")
  && c.LastName.Equals("Becker")
  select c).AsEnumerable<PersonInformation>().FirstOrDefault();
```

This code snippet does not raise an exception because we used `EnableScanInQuery`.

Setting index precisions

Before we dive into specifying and manipulating index paths, let's take a look at setting index precisions. Index precisions define how accurate an index is. Setting the precision to the maximum enables DocumentDB to query efficiently and search for the right result. Inserting documents will cause additional overhead because the index also needs to be updated. Setting the maximum precision comes at a cost; it maximizes the index storage space but the index search will be very precise. Setting the string index precision to 5, for example, means that more records will map to the same index entry. This saves index storage but executing the query might need to iterate over more documents and probably use more request units as well. The following code snippet will set the index precision for a typical path in our `PersonInformation` class:

```
//tell documentDB to set the precision to -1 (meaning maximum
precision) for all
  //properties underneath /HomeAutomationDevices (for all documents)
  collection.IndexingPolicy.IncludedPaths.Add(
  new IncludedPath
  {
    Path = "/HomeAutomationDevices/*",
    Indexes = new Collection<Index> {
    new RangeIndex(DataType.String) { Precision = -1 },
    new RangeIndex(DataType.Number) { Precision = -1 }
  }
});

  //instead of creating a collection with this indexingpolicy
precision we update the current one
  await client.ReplaceDocumentCollectionAsync(collection);

  //use this code to create a new collection with the indexing policy
precision
  //await client.CreateDocumentCollectionAsync(database.SelfLink,
collection);
```

The result of running this code snippet is that the already existing collection is updated with the index precision. Setting this index precision for all properties inside the `/HomeAutomationDevices` path enables precise indexing (maximum precision).

> When creating a collection, the index precision for all paths is set to maximum by default. The spatial index cannot be overridden and always uses the default index precision.

Varying the index precision and investigating the number of request units used gives you a good balance between performance and costs.

> If you need to use OrderBy in your queries on string properties, you need to make sure the index precision is set to the maximum (-1).

Reapplying index configuration might take some time to be committed. In order to track the progress, DocumentDB offers an easy to use capability that is part of the ReadDocumentCollectionAsync method. The following code snippet will help you to track the progress:

```
long waitTime = 500; //0.5 seconds to wait for next call
long progress = 0;

//do while progress is not 100 yet
while (progress >= 0 && progress < 100)
{
    ResourceResponse<DocumentCollection> collectionReadResponse =
await client.ReadDocumentCollectionAsync(findCollection.SelfLink);
    progress = collectionReadResponse.IndexTransformationProgress;

    await Task.Delay(TimeSpan.FromMilliseconds(waitTime));
}
```

This piece of code checks the IndexTransformationProgress and keeps tracking it until it reaches 100 percent.

Manipulating paths in indexes

Besides offering the three index modes, DocumentDB also has the capability of really fine-graining and controlling the way the indexing process is executed. This gives us the ability to explicitly opt-in and opt-out for documents and/or paths inside documents (paths).

All index paths, by default, start with the / character and end with a * or ? character. Ending the index path with a * symbol indicates recursion, which means all nodes under this specific node are included in the index path. Using the ? symbol indicates that only the designed node is undergoing the index change.

Take a look at the following queries to get a better understanding of using the wildcards:

Path	Usage
`/*`	This is the default value when creating a collection. It means it is recursive for the whole document.

`/HomeAutomationDevices/*`	This means everything recursive in the `HomeAutomationDevices` subtree.
	
	For example:
	
	`Select * from coll c where`
	`c.HomeAutomationDevices.NumberOfDevices`
	`= 10`

`/HomeAutomationDevices/?`	This only applies to the `HomeAutomationDevices` node.
	
	`Select * from coll c where`
	`c.HomeAutomationDevices != null`

`/HomeAutomationDevices/ []/*`	This applies to the whole subtree and enables joining and scalar operations.

Setting different index types

DocumentDB supports three types of indexes:

- **Hash**: This index kind supports efficient equality (=) and `JOIN` queries
- **Range**: This index kind supports efficient equality, range queries and `OrderBy` queries (`OrderBy` requires a precision of `-1`)
- **Spatial**: This index kind supports efficient spatial queries like `Distance`

The following table outlines some basic queries of these indexes:

Index	Example
Hash	`Select * from p where p.LastName = "Becker"`
Range	`Select * from p where NumberOfHomeAutomationDevices > 10` `Select * from p order by p.LastName`
Spatial	`Select * from p where ST_DISTANCE(p.Location, <POINT>) ,` `100`

We know that DocumentDB returns an error if a range query is supplied without a range index. Also, using spatial queries on properties where no spatial index is provided has the same behavior. This error contains information that a full scan is needed for this query. To be able to execute these queries, we need to set the `EnableScanInQuery`.

Configuring index paths

In the previous section, we discussed index paths and how to specify them. Now, we will discuss more about precision, data types, and index types. The following code snippets and inline comments will teach us about settings precisions, using datatypes, index types, and how to include or exclude properties.

The following snippet will explicitly exclude a document from indexing:

```
Document created = await client.CreateDocumentAsync(collection.
SelfLink, new
  PersonInformation
  {
    FirstName = "John",
    LastName = "Doe",
    DateOfBirth = new DateEpoch
    {
      Date = DateTime.UtcNow
    }
  },
  new RequestOptions
  {
    IndexingDirective = IndexingDirective.Exclude
  });
```

The following snippet will turn indexing off for a collection and prove this by adding a document and try to search for it after insertion:

```
//this snippets shows how to include explicitly. This is only possible
if the IndexingPolicy.Automatic is set to False
  //on the collection level
  collection.IndexingPolicy.Automatic = false;
  //make sure the collection has no indexing policy
  await client.ReplaceDocumentCollectionAsync(collection);
```

```
// Create a simple document with and try to query for it later
Document nonIndexedDocument = await client.
CreateDocumentAsync(collection.SelfLink,
  new PersonInformation
  {
    FirstName = "Jane",
    LastName = "CannotBeIndexed"
  });
```

```
PersonInformation doc = (from p in client.CreateDocumentQuery<Person
Information>(collection.DocumentsLink)
  where p.LastName == "CannotBeIndexed"
  select p).AsEnumerable().FirstOrDefault();
//doc should be null since it cannot be found through an index
if (null == doc)
{
  Console.WriteLine("As expected, the document cannot be found");
}
```

We can do the same for a non-indexed collection, and then explicitly add a document to be indexed anyway:

```
Document IndexedDocument = await client.
CreateDocumentAsync(collection.SelfLink,
  new PersonInformation
  {
    FirstName = "Jane",
    LastName = "ExplicitlyIndexed"
  },
  new RequestOptions
  {
    IndexingDirective = IndexingDirective.Include
  }
);
```

```
// Query for the document again and this time we should find it
because we manually included the document in the index
PersonInformation explicitlyIndexedDoc = (from p in client.CreateDoc
umentQuery<PersonInformation>(collection.DocumentsLink)
  where p.LastName == "ExplicitlyIndexed"
  select p).AsEnumerable().FirstOrDefault();
```

```
//doc should be null since it cannot be found through an index
if (null != explicitlyIndexedDoc)
{
   Console.WriteLine("As expected, this document is found through the
explicit index.");
}
```

Range indexes are used to order our result set. In this code snippet, we explicitly set the range index and precision on the `LastName` property to be able to sort the results on `LastName`:

```
collection.IndexingPolicy.IncludedPaths.Add(new IncludedPath
{
  Path = "/LastName/?",
  Indexes = new Collection<Index>()
  {
    new RangeIndex(DataType.Number) { Precision = -1 },
    new RangeIndex(DataType.String) { Precision = -1 }
  }
});

collection = await client.ReplaceDocumentCollectionAsync(collecti
on);
//create two documents that will be subject to the OrderBy
await client.CreateDocumentAsync(collection.SelfLink,
new PersonInformation
{
  FirstName = "Jane",
  LastName = "OrderbyA"
});
await client.CreateDocumentAsync(collection.SelfLink,
new PersonInformation
{
  FirstName = "Jane",
  LastName = "OrderbyB"
});

// Now ordering against LastName is allowed.
var docs = (from p in client.CreateDocumentQuery<PersonInformation>(
collection.DocumentsLink)
  orderby p.LastName
  select p).AsEnumerable();
//using the same query trying to use OrderBy on FirstName simple
returns an empty result set
```

In this section, we saw how to include or exclude specific indexing for documents or the entire collection.

> Try excluding paths from the collection to disable range queries on the `LastName` property.

Setting the index precision

In this section, we will see how setting the index precision affects querying. The effect of setting the precision to less than the maximum is less usage of index storage but more overhead on querying the documents since multiple documents will be in the same range. The code is as follows:

```
//setting the max precision (-1)
collection.IndexingPolicy.IncludedPaths.Clear();
collection.IndexingPolicy.Automatic = false;
collection = await client.ReplaceDocumentCollectionAsync(collecti
on);
collection.IndexingPolicy.IncludedPaths.Add(new IncludedPath
{
  Path = "/LastName/?",
  Indexes = new Collection<Index>()
  {
    new RangeIndex(DataType.Number) { Precision = -1 },
    new RangeIndex(DataType.String) { Precision = -1 }
  }
});

collection = await client.ReplaceDocumentCollectionAsync(collecti
on);
//create two documents that will be subject to the OrderBy
var result = await client.CreateDocumentAsync(collection.SelfLink,
new PersonInformation
{
  FirstName = "John",
  LastName = "MaxPrecision"

});
var result2 = await client.CreateDocumentAsync(collection.SelfLink,
new PersonInformation
{
```

```
      FirstName = "John",
      LastName = "MaxPrecision2"


  });
  //print request units for this insert
  Console.WriteLine("RU's needed:" + result.RequestCharge.ToString());

  //wipe the paths again (the standard ones remain)
  collection.IndexingPolicy.IncludedPaths.Clear();
  collection = await client.ReplaceDocumentCollectionAsync(collecti
on);
  //precision to 2 bytes only
  collection.IndexingPolicy.IncludedPaths.Add(new IncludedPath
  {
    Path = "/LastName/?",
    Indexes = new Collection<Index>()
    {
      new RangeIndex(DataType.Number) { Precision = -1 },
      new RangeIndex(DataType.String) { Precision = 2 }
    }
  });
  collection = await client.ReplaceDocumentCollectionAsync(collecti
on);

  result = await client.CreateDocumentAsync(collection.SelfLink,
  new PersonInformation
  {
    FirstName = "John",
    LastName = "LessPrecision"
  });
  result2 = await client.CreateDocumentAsync(collection.SelfLink,
  new PersonInformation
  {
    FirstName = "John",
    LastName = "LessPrecision2"
  });
  //print request units for this insert
  Console.WriteLine("RU's needed:" + result2.RequestCharge.
ToString());
```

This snippet demonstrates the use of setting the precision. It also shows how to replace the existing `IncludedPaths` property by clearing it and saving the collection. This is good for demonstration purposes, since we do not need to create new collections for every example.

Partitioning data

As we saw in *Chapter 1, Getting Started with DocumentDB*, DocumentDB has limits on its resources. A maximum of 10 GB per collection and maximum requests units per collection is set to 2,500 per second. To be able to go above these limits and reach a truly high scale, we need to partition our data by using sharding. For more information on the sharding pattern, please visit `https://msdn.microsoft.com/en-us/library/dn589797.aspx`.

Collections in DocumentDB are both logical and physical containers. Triggers and stored procedures do not go beyond these boundaries when it comes to transactions.

This section will discuss how to use sharding. The best sharding techniques are based on how our data is formatted and accessed. Basically, there are two sharding techniques:

- Hash partitioning
- Range partitioning

Using hash partitioning

When we use hash partitioning, partitions are assigned based on the outcome of a hash function. This will allow us to distribute all requests and data evenly across partitions. This scenario is helpful in cases when a large amount of telemetry data of an IoT scenario is being stored in DocumentDB. To enable this, we need to use the `HashPartitionResolver` class.

The following code snippet demonstrates how to set up hash partitioning. For this snippet, we create two separate collections that will play a role inside the partitioning logic:

```
// Initialize a HashPartitionResolver using the "LastName" property
and the two collection self-links.
  HashPartitionResolver hashResolver = new HashPartitionResolver(
  u => ((PersonInformation)u).LastName,
  new string[] { collection1.SelfLink, collection2.SelfLink });

  // Register the PartitionResolver with the database since the
partitioning takes place on a database level
  client.PartitionResolvers[database.SelfLink] = hashResolver;
```

This piece of code creates a `HashPartitionResolver` that will be used on two collections.

```
//the partitionresolver hashes the lastname  to determine which
collection to use
  //now query against the partition
  var query = client.CreateDocumentQuery<PersonInformation>(
  database.SelfLink, null, hashResolver.GetPartitionKey(janePi))
  .Where(u => u.LastName == "Doe");

  var janeInformation = query.AsEnumerable().FirstOrDefault();
```

This code snippet directly uses the `hashResolver` to get the hash value of `janePi` (which is an instance of the `PersonInformation` class). The following code snippet returns the exact same result but without specifying the resolver directly:

```
query = client.CreateDocumentQuery<PersonInformation>(database.
SelfLink)
  .Where(u => u.LastName == "Doe");
```

Using range partitioning

When we use range partitioning, partitions (collections) are assigned based on the partition. This scenario can be applied, for example, when using timestamp properties to store documents with a certain date interval to reside in one partition. You could store all data that is created in a month in a designated partition. To enable this, we need to use the `RangePartitionResolver` class.

The following code snippet will set up range partitioning:

```
//now execute range partitioning on LastName
  RangePartitionResolver<string> rangePartitionResolver = new RangePar
titionResolver<string>("LastName",
  new Dictionary<Range<string>, string>()
  {
    { new Range<string>("A", "M"), collection1.SelfLink },
    { new Range<string>("N", "Z"), collection2.SelfLink },
  });
  //rangepartitionresolver with the database since the partitioning
takes place on a database level
  client.PartitionResolvers[database.SelfLink] =
rangePartitionResolver;
```

This snippet creates a `RangePartitionResolver`, enabling two ranges. Last names starting with A-M will be stored inside a partition (`collection1`) and last names starting with N-Z will be stored inside `collection2`.

The following code snippet queries for `John` in two different ways. First, using the default `CreateDocumentQuery` method and then using the `partitionResolver` explicitly:

```
//find John
   query = client.CreateDocumentQuery<PersonInformation>(database.
SelfLink).Where(
   u => u.LastName == "Something"); //goes to first partition
   foreach (PersonInformation pi in query)
   {
      Console.WriteLine(pi.LastName);
   }
   //find John using the partitionresolver directly
   query = client.CreateDocumentQuery<PersonInformation>(database.
SelfLink, null,
   rangePartitionResolver.GetPartitionKey(johnDocument))
   .Where(u => u.LastName == "Something");
   //get John
   PersonInformation piJohn = query.AsEnumerable().FirstOrDefault();
   Console.WriteLine(String.Format("John {0} was found!", piJohn.
LastName));
```

This section provided some insight on using partitioning with DocumentDB. There are many ways of defining partitions. It is also possible to let your database grow with more collections if needed.

> Try creating a custom `PartitionResolver` that creates collections in flight. When documents are added and the partitions fill up equally, it enables growth in a number of partitions.

Managing performance

DocumentDB offers information about performance. We can use these to fine-tune our indexing policy and make the best decision on performance versus storage.

We can check the `ResourceResponse` class to get more information about the used RUs for a specific operation but also on other metrics. The following table outlines some of the properties of the `ResourceResponse` class that can be used to gather some metadata on the resource requests we perform:

Property	Description
CollectionSizeUsage	This returns the current size of a collection in kilobytes. This can be useful to detect if we are about to exceed the maximum of the collection. Based on this we can shard, scale out, or perform some other operation to prevent adding a document from failing.
CollectionUsage	This specifies the number of collections present in the account.
CurrentResourceQuotaUsage	This returns the current size of the entity involved. This one can be useful to see if the documents we are adding are not too large, which might affect performance or limit the number of documents that can be stored. Using images or other binary streams can cause this behavior.
IndexTransformationProgress	If an index transformation has been started (like we did in this chapter), we should definitely check this property to make sure the indexing process is finished before we start adding new documents.
RequestCharge	This specifies the number of RUs that were consumed for this specific operation.

We can get the `ResourceResponse` using the following code snippet:

```
var result2 = await client.CreateDocumentAsync(collection.SelfLink,
  new PersonInformation
  {
    FirstName = "John",
    LastName = "ResourceResponse"

});
//print request units for this insert
Console.WriteLine("RU's needed:" + result.RequestCharge.ToString());
```

Different factors influence the number of RUs that are needed for different types of operation:

- **Number of properties:** When all properties are indexed (default behavior), the number of RUs needed for an insert or update increases as the number of properties increase

- **Size of the document:** A large document consumes more RUs for reading and writing than a small document

- **Consistency level**: When the consistency level of your collection is strong or has bounded staleness, more RUs are needed to read documents

- **Indexing**: Turning off automatic indexing for your document(s) decreases the number of RUs needed

- **Indexed properties**: Only indexing some of the properties of your documents decreases the consumption rate of request units as well

The number of RUs consumed by triggers, stored procedures, and user-defined functions depends on the complexity of the code.

Using transactions

Transactions inside DocumentDB are applicable only in server-side code. This means that building a transactional system can be achieved, for example, by writing stored procedures. Since stored procedures exist on a collection level, transactions can only span one collection, and adding or modifying documents across collections is not supported at the time of writing.

DocumentDB handles all logic that is running inside a stored procedure or trigger a transaction explicitly. There is no need to start and commit a transaction whatsoever. This is explicitly managed by the execution engine of DocumentDB. If an exception is raised inside the stored procedure or trigger, the entire transaction is aborted accordingly. This prevents inconsistent data by default. A simple example of a transaction in a stored procedure is shown in the following snippet:

```
function TransactionExample(document) {
  var collection = getContext().getCollection();
  var collectionLink = collection.getSelfLink();

  collection.createDocument(collectionLink, document);
```

```
    //if document contains rollback property then throw exception
    if (document.LastName == "NoTransaction") {
        throw "Exception, we do not want to continue. The document created
is rolled back.";
    }
}
```

This simple stored procedure takes a document as an argument and checks the `LastName` property of the document. If the `LastName` equals `NoTransaction`, the stored procedure will throw an exception and the document that was already created will be rolled back. You can test this stored procedure with the following C# snippet (not possible to test in the Azure portal yet):

```
//check if the sp is already there
var storedProcedure = client.CreateStoredProcedureQuery(collection.
SelfLink).Where(u => u.Id == "TransactionExample").
AsEnumerable().FirstOrDefault();
if ( storedProcedure == null)
{
    storedProcedure = new StoredProcedure
    {
        Id = "TransactionExample",
        //the body is in the storedprocedure.js file
        Body = File.ReadAllText("StoredProcedure.js")
    };
    storedProcedure = await client.CreateStoredProcedureAsync(collecti
on.SelfLink, storedProcedure);
}
//create two documents. One that will succeed and one that will be
rolled back in the sp
PersonInformation success = new PersonInformation
{
    FirstName = "John",
    LastName = "Transaction"
};

PersonInformation fail = new PersonInformation
{
    FirstName = "John",
    LastName = "NoTransaction"
};
```

```
//execute stored procedure and verify that it successful
(transaction!).
var scriptResult = await client.ExecuteStoredProcedureAsync<dynamic>(s
toredProcedure.SelfLink, success);
try
{
  //execute stored procedure and verify that fails (transaction!).
  scriptResult = await client.ExecuteStoredProcedureAsync<dynamic>(sto
redProcedure.SelfLink, fail);
}
catch (Exception ex)
{
  Console.WriteLine("Stored procedure failed:" + ex.Message);
}
```

The first call to the stored procedure is successful, while the second one raises an exception because of the `LastName` property.

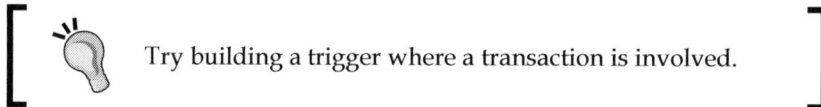

[🔦 Try building a trigger where a transaction is involved.]

Setting consistency levels

DocumentDB offers different levels of consistency. Again, this is a matter of balancing between performance, consistency, and latency. DocumentDB offers four levels of consistency, each with its own characteristics.

Consistency levels can only be set on user defined resources such as documents and triggers. By default, all system resources such as databases and collections are strongly consistency enabled. The following types of consistency levels are available:

- Strong
- Bounded staleness
- Session
- Eventual

Setting the consistency level can be accomplished using the designated SDKs or the Azure portal, as shown in the following screenshot:

Using strong consistency

Strong consistency means that a write to a collection, database, or some other user defined resource is visible only after it is committed by the majority of the replicas. This means that a client cannot face an uncommitted write and DocumentDB always guarantees to return the latest write that was successful.

This consistency level provides the highest level of data consistency. The downside is that it also offers the lowest level of performance.

Using bounded staleness consistency

Bounded staleness consistency means that reads might lag behind writes. The read is confirmed by the majority of replicas and, therefore, the response of the read request specifies the "relative freshness".

This consistency levels offers a more predictable behavior for read consistency (since the majority wins) and it offers the lowest latency writes (since these occur immediately). Because the reads are being confirmed by the majority only, the latency for reading is not the lowest that is offered.

Using session consistency

Session consistency applies only to the client that is involved. Only the client performing the operations is guaranteed the have the latest writes and reads of all data. This is achieved because a read request is executed against a replica that is capable of serving the right version of the data. A session cookie is used to achieve this behavior.

This level of consistency provides a very predictable consistency for reading during a session (obviously) and it offers the lowest latency on writing (since it writes to the "session-enabled" replica only).

Using eventual staleness consistency

This level of consistency is the weakest consistency level provided. Clients may be offered data that is older than earlier reads. All replicas will eventually be consistent with each other if no further writes are executed. If writes keep occurring, none of the replicas will ever be consistent at the same time. This is old data and might be served for a read request.

This type of consistency has the worst read consistency but the lowest latency on writing and reading data.

Summary

In this chapter we have learned how to influence the way DocumentDB indexes our data. We changed index paths and precision and changed the index mode that is used. We saw how to use spatial data and how to explicitly turn indexing on and off for documents.

Next, we saw how to partition our data and how to use the designated resolvers to enable proper partitioning. Partitioning is useful to distribute the load in case we run out of request units or in case we run out of storage.

We have learned the basics of transactions for DocumentDB and we saw how transactions are handled inside a stored procedure. Finally we have learned how consistency levels can be used and the impact of the different types of consistency levels.

The next chapter will outline an IoT scenario and how DocumentDB can play a role. It will also demonstrate how to combine DocumentDB together with other Azure service offerings to build a mature enterprise solution.

8

Putting Your Database at the Heart of Azure Solutions

This chapter describes building a real scenario around an Internet of Things scenario. We will use the different techniques we saw in the previous chapter and combine these with existing features from the Microsoft Azure platform. This scenario will build a basic Internet of Things platform that will help to accelerate building your own.

In this chapter, we will cover the following:

- Have a look at a fictitious scenario
- Learn how to combine Azure components with DocumentDB
- Demonstrate how to migrate data to DocumentDB

Introducing an Internet of Things scenario

Before we start exploring different capabilities to support a real-life scenario, we will briefly explain the scenario we will use throughout this chapter.

IoT Inc.

IoT, Inc. is a fictitious start-up company that is planning to build solutions in the Internet of Things domain. The first solution they will build is a registration hub, in which IoT devices can be registered. These devices can be diverse, ranging from home automation devices to devices that control traffic lights and street lights. The main use case for this solution is offering the capability for devices to register themselves against a hub.

The hub will be built with DocumentDB as its core component and a web API to expose this functionality. Before devices can register themselves, they need to be whitelisted in order to prevent malicious devices from registering.

In the following screenshot, we see the high-level design of the registration requirement:

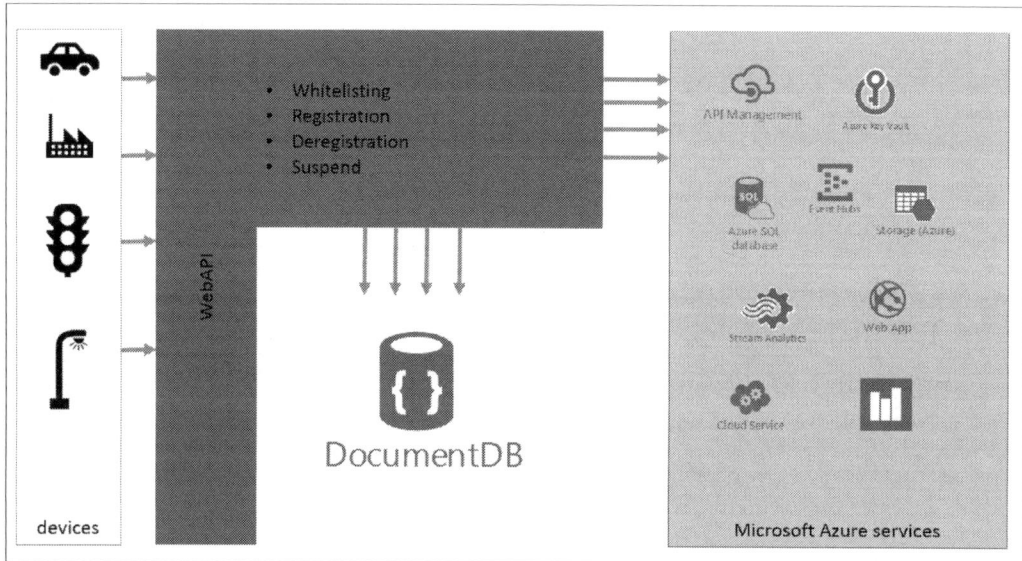

The first version of the solution contains the following components:

- A Web API containing methods to whitelist, register, unregister, and suspend devices
- DocumentDB, containing all the device information, including information regarding other Microsoft Azure resources
- Event Hub, a Microsoft Azure asset that enables scalable publish-subscribe mechanism to ingress and egress millions of events per second
- Power BI, Microsoft's online offering to expose reporting capabilities and the ability to share reports

Obviously, we will focus on the core of the solution, which is DocumentDB, but it is nice to touch some of the Azure components, as well to see how well they co-operate and how easy it is to set up a demonstration for IoT scenarios. The devices on the left-hand side are chosen randomly and will be mimicked by an emulator written in C#.

The Web API will expose the functionality required to let devices register themselves at the solution and start sending data afterwards (which will be ingested to the Event Hub and reported using Power BI).

Technical requirements

To be able to service potentially millions of devices, it is necessary that registration request from a device is being stored in a separate collection based on the country where the device is located or manufactured.

- Every device is being modeled in the same way, whereas additional metadata can be provided upon registration or afterwards when updating.

- To achieve country-based partitioning, we will create a custom `PartitionResolver` to achieve this goal.

- To extend the basic security model, we will reduce the amount of sensitive information in our configuration files.

- Enhance searching capabilities because we want to service multiple types of devices each with their own metadata and device-specific information. Querying on all the information is desired to support full-text search and enable users to quickly search and find their devices.

Designing the model

Every device is being modeled similarly to be able to service multiple types of devices. The device model contains at least the device ID and a location. Furthermore, the device model contains a dictionary where additional device properties can be stored. The next code snippet shows the device model:

```
[JsonProperty("id")]
        public string DeviceId { get; set; }
        [JsonProperty("location")]
        public Point Location { get; set; }
        //practically store any metadata information for this device
        [JsonProperty("metadata")]
        public IDictionary<string, object> MetaData { get; set; }
```

> The Location property is of type Microsoft.Azure.Documents.Spatial.Point because we want to run spatial queries later on in this section, for example, getting all the devices within 10 kilometers of a building.

Building a custom partition resolver

To meet the first technical requirement (partition data based on the country), we need to build a custom partition resolver. To be able to build one, we need to implement the IPartitionResolver interface and add some logic. The resolver will take the Location property of the device model and retrieve the country that corresponds with the latitude and longitude provided upon registration.

In the following code snippet, you will see the full implementation of the GeographyPartitionResolver class:

```
public class GeographyPartitionResolver : IPartitionResolver
    {
        private readonly DocumentClient _client;
        private readonly BingMapsHelper _helper;
        private readonly Database _database;

        public GeographyPartitionResolver(DocumentClient client,
Database database)
        {
            _client = client;
            _database = database;
            _helper = new BingMapsHelper();
        }
        public object GetPartitionKey(object document)
        {
            //get the country for this document
            //document should be of type DeviceModel
            if (document.GetType() == typeof(DeviceModel))
            {
                //get the Location and translate to country
                var country = _helper.GetCountryByLatitudeLongitude(
                    (document as DeviceModel).Location.Position.
Latitude,
                    (document as DeviceModel).Location.Position.
Longitude);
                return country;
            }
            return String.Empty;
        }
```

```
    public string ResolveForCreate(object partitionKey)
    {
        //get the country for this partitionkey
        //check if there is a collection for the country found

        var countryCollection = _client.CreateDocumentCollectionQu
ery(database.SelfLink).
            ToList().Where(cl => cl.Id.Equals(partitionKey.
ToString())).FirstOrDefault();
        if (null == countryCollection)
        {
            countryCollection = new DocumentCollection { Id =
partitionKey.ToString() };
            countryCollection =
                _client.CreateDocumentCollectionAsync(_database.
SelfLink, countryCollection).Result;
        }
        return countryCollection.SelfLink;
    }


    /// <summary>
    /// Returns a list of collectionlinks for the designated
partitionkey (one per country)
    /// </summary>
    /// <param name="partitionKey"></param>
    /// <returns></returns>
    public IEnumerable<string> ResolveForRead(object partitionKey)
    {
        var countryCollection = _client.
CreateDocumentCollectionQuery(_database.SelfLink).
            ToList().Where(cl => cl.Id.Equals(partitionKey.
ToString())).FirstOrDefault();

        return new List<string>
        {
            countryCollection.SelfLink
        };
    }
}
```

In order to have the DocumentDB client use this custom `PartitionResolver`, we need to assign it. The code is as follows:

```
GeographyPartitionResolver resolver = new GeographyPartitionResolver(d
ocDbClient, _database);

docDbClient.PartitionResolvers[_database.SelfLink] = resolver;
//Adding a typical device and have the resolver sort out what //
country is involved and whether or not the collection already //exists
(and create a collection for the country if needed), use //the next
code snippet.
var deviceInAmsterdam = new DeviceModel
        {
            DeviceId = Guid.NewGuid().ToString(),
            Location = new Point(4.8951679, 52.3702157)
        };

Document modelAmsDocument = docDbClient.CreateDocumentAsync(_database.
SelfLink,
            deviceInAmsterdam).Result;
        //get all the devices in Amsterdam
    var doc = docDbClient.CreateDocumentQuery<DeviceModel>(
            _database.SelfLink, null, resolver.GetPartitionKey(dev
iceInAmsterdam));
```

Now that we have created a country-based `PartitionResolver`, we can start working on the Web API that exposes the registration method.

Building the Web API

A Web API is an online service that can be used by any client running any framework that supports the HTTP programming stack. Currently, REST is a way of interacting with APIs, so that we will build a REST API. Building a good API should aim for platform independence. A well-designed API should also be able to extend and evolve without affecting existing clients.

First, we need to whitelist the devices that should be able to register themselves against our device registry. The whitelist should at least contain a device ID, a unique identifier for a device that is used for match during the whitelisting process. A good candidate for a device ID is the MAC address of the device or some random GUID.

Registering a device

The registration Web API contains a POST method that does the actual registration. First, it creates access to an Event Hub (not explained here) and stores the credentials needed inside the DocumentDB document. The document is then created inside the designated collection (based on the location). To learn more about Event Hubs, please visit https://azure.microsoft.com/en-us/services/event-hubs/.

```
[Route("api/registration")]
        [HttpPost]
        public async Task<IHttpActionResult> Post([FromBody]
DeviceModel value)
        {
            //add the device to the designated documentDB collection
(based on country)
            try
            {
var serviceUri = ServiceBusEnvironment.CreateServiceUri("sb",
serviceBusNamespace,
                    String.Format("{0}/publishers/{1}", "telemetry",
value.DeviceId))
                    .ToString()
                    .Trim('/');
                var sasToken = SharedAccessSignatureTokenProvider.GetS
haredAccessSignature(EventHubKeyName,
                    EventHubKey, serviceUri, TimeSpan.FromDays(365 *
100)); // hundred years will do
                //this token can be used by the device to send
telemetry
                //this token and the eventhub name will be saved with
the metadata of the document to be saved to DocumentDB
                value.MetaData.Add("Namespace", serviceBusNamespace);
                value.MetaData.Add("EventHubName", "telemetry");
                value.MetaData.Add("EventHubToken", sasToken);
                var document = await docDbClient.CreateDocumentAsync(_
database.SelfLink, value);
                return Created(document.ContentLocation, value);
}
            catch (Exception ex)
            {
                return InternalServerError(ex);
            }
        }
```

After this registration call, the right credentials on the Event Hub will have been created for this specific device. The device is now able to ingress data to the Event Hub and have consumers like Power BI consume the data and present it.

Event Hubs is a highly scalable publish-subscribe event ingestor. It can collect millions of events per second so that you can process and analyze the massive amounts of data produced by your connected devices and applications. Once collected into Event Hubs, you can transform and store the data by using any real-time analytics provider or with batching/storage adapters.

> At the time of writing, Microsoft announced the release of Azure IoT Suite and IoT Hubs. These solutions offer Internet of Things capabilities as a service and are well-suited to building our scenario as well.

Increasing search capabilities

We have seen how to query our documents and retrieve the information we need. For this approach, we need to understand the DocumentDB SQL language. Microsoft has an online offering that enables full-text search called Azure Search service. This feature enables us to perform full-text searches and it also includes search behaviors similar to search engines. We could also benefit from so called type-ahead query suggestions based on the input of a user. Imagine a search box on our IoT Inc. portal that offers free text searching while the user types and searches for devices that include any of the search terms on the fly. Azure Search runs on Azure; therefore, it is scalable and can easily be upgraded to offer more search and storage capacity.

Azure Search stores all your data inside an index, offering full-text search capabilities on your data.

Setting up Azure Search

Setting up Azure Search is pretty straightforward and can be done by using the REST API it offers or on the Azure portal. We will set up the Azure Search service through the portal and later on, we will utilize the REST API to start configuring our search service.

We set up the Azure Search service through the Azure portal (`http://portal.azure.com`). Find the Search service and fill out some information. In the following screenshot, we can see how we have created the free tier for Azure Search:

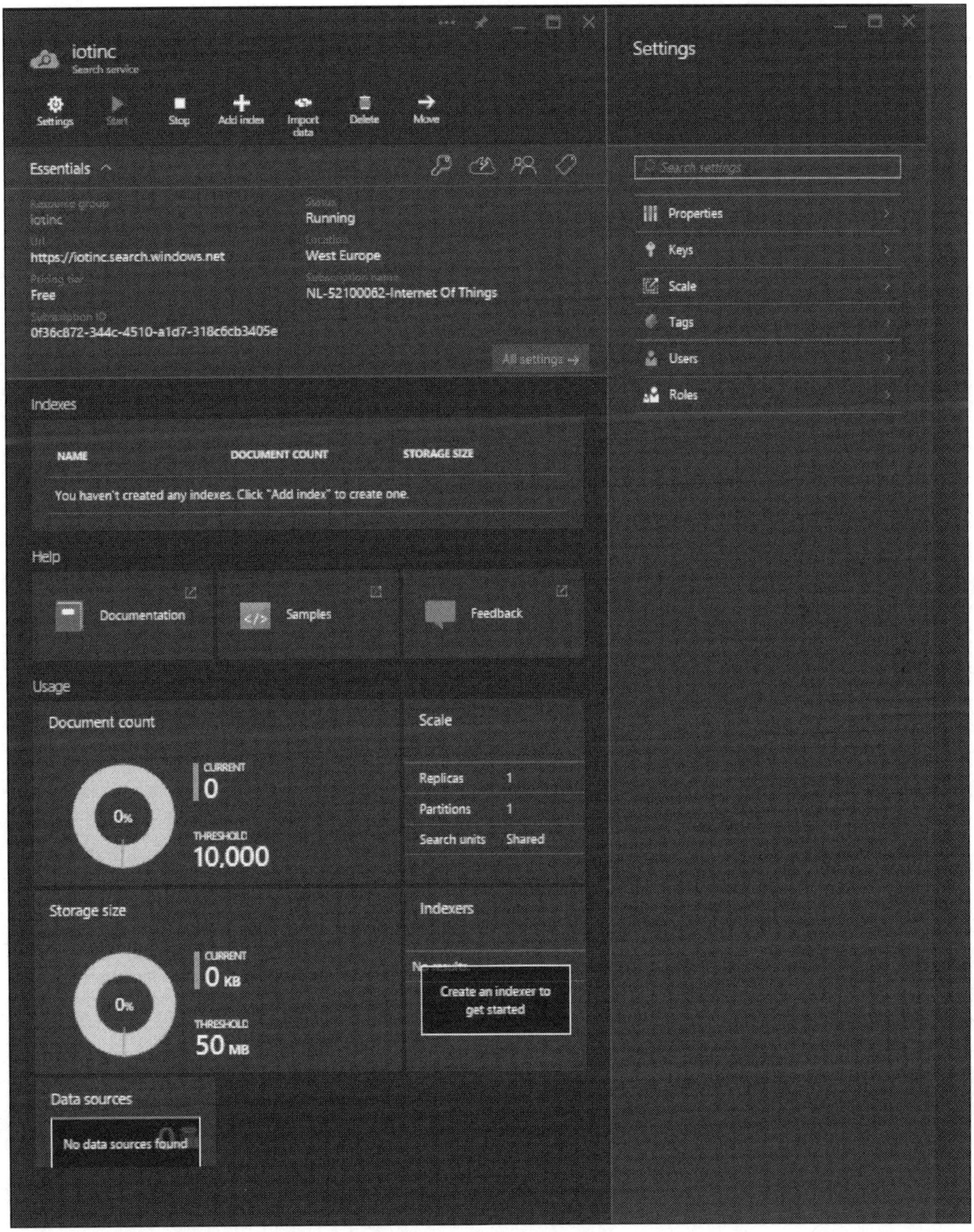

You can see that we use the Free tier for this scenario and that there are no data sources configured yet. We will do this now by using the REST API.

We will use the REST API, since it offers more insight on how the whole concept works. We use Fiddler to create a new data source inside our search environment. The following screenshot shows how to use Fiddler to create a data source and add a DocumentDB collection:

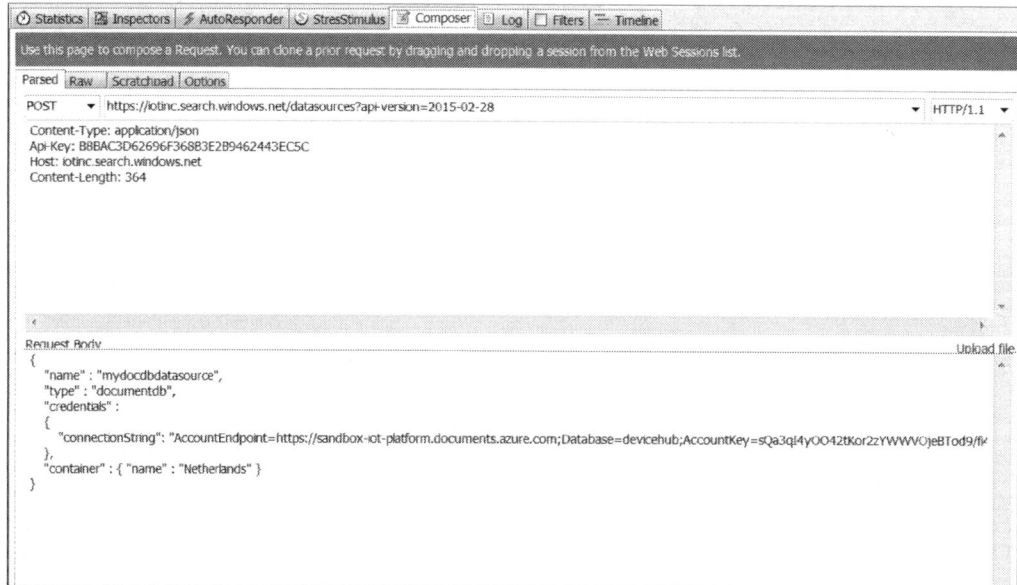

In the **Composer** window of Fiddler, you can see we need to POST a payload to the Search service we created earlier. The Api-Key is mandatory and also set the content type to be JSON. Inside the body of the request, the connection information to our DocumentDB environment is needed as well the collection we want to add (in this case, the Netherlands).

Now that we have added the collection, it is time to create an Azure Search index. Again, we use Fiddler for this purpose. Since we are using the free tier of Azure Search, we can only add five indexes at most. For this scenario, we add an index on ID (device ID), location, and metadata. At the time of writing, Azure Search does not support complex types.

Note that the metadata node is represented as a collection of strings.

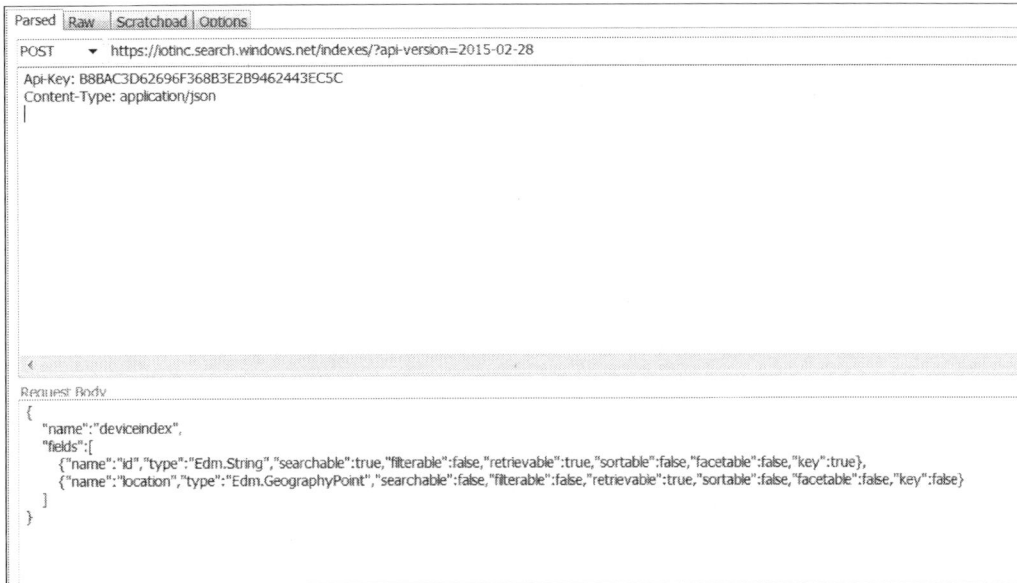

We could check in the portal to see if the creation of the index was successful. Go to the Search blade and select the Search service we have just created. You can check the indexes part to see whether the index was actually created.

The next step is to create an indexer. An indexer connects the index with the provided data source.

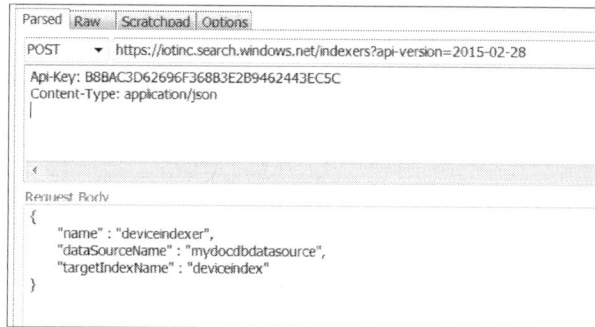

Creating this indexer takes some time. You can check in the portal if the indexing process was successful. We actually find that documents are part of the index now.

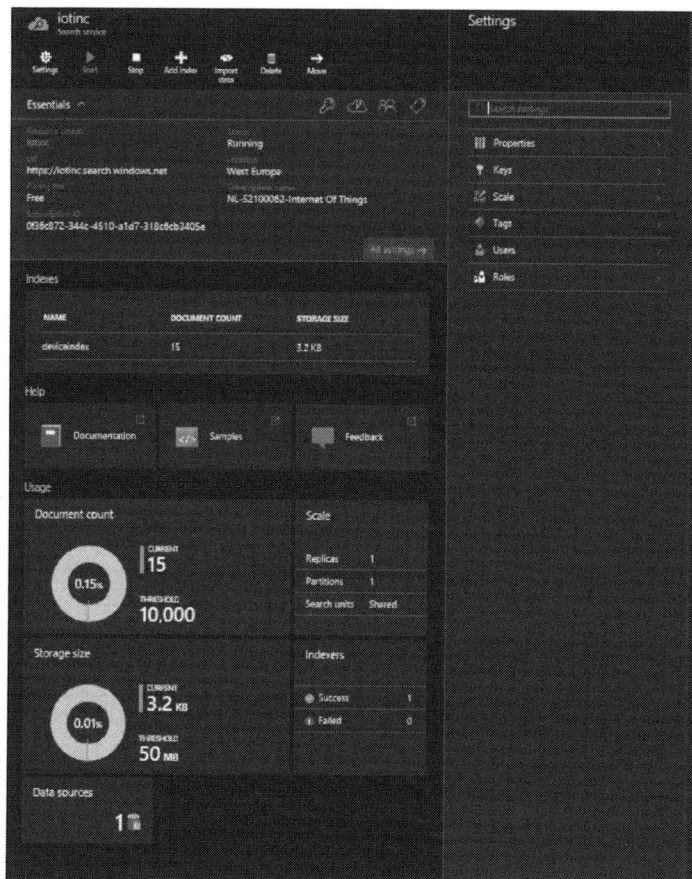

If your indexer needs to process thousands of documents, it might take some time for the indexing process to finish. You can check the progress of the indexer using the REST API again:

```
https://<namespace>.search.windows.net/
indexers/<name of your indexer>/status?api-
versoin=2015-02-28
```

Using this REST call returns the result of the indexing process and indicates if it is still running and also shows if there are any errors. Errors could be caused by documents that do not have the id property available.

The final step involves testing to check whether the indexing works. We will search for a device ID, as shown in the next screenshot:

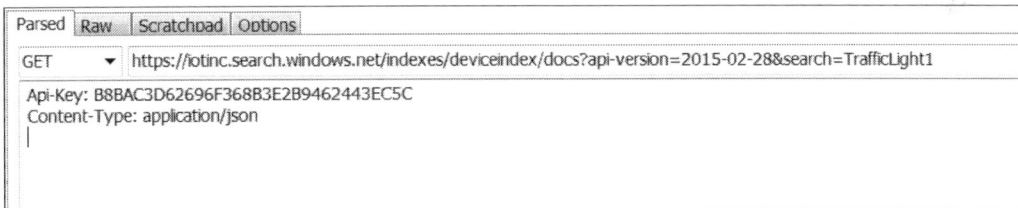

Parsed	Raw	Scratchpad	Options

GET ▼ https://iotinc.search.windows.net/indexes/deviceindex/docs?api-version=2015-02-28&search=TrafficLight1

Api-Key: B8BAC3D62696F368B3E2B9462443EC5C
Content-Type: application/json

In the **Inspector** tab, we can check for the results. It actually returns the correct document, also containing the location field. The metadata is missing because complex JSON is not supported (yet) at the time of writing.

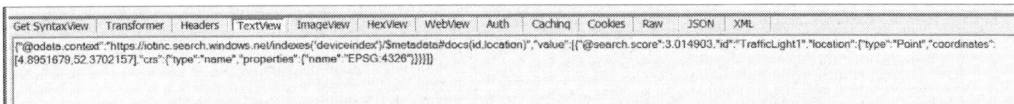

Get SyntaxView	Transformer	Headers	TextView	ImageView	HexView	WebView	Auth	Caching	Cookies	Raw	JSON	XML

{"@odata.context":"https://iotinc.search.windows.net/indexes('deviceindex')/$metadata#docs(id,location)","value":[{"@search.score":3.014903,"id":"TrafficLight1","location":{"type":"Point","coordinates":[4.8951679,52.3702157],"crs":{"type":"name","properties":{"name":"EPSG:4326"}}}}]}

Indexing complex JSON types is not supported yet. It is possible to add SQL queries to the data source. We could explicitly add a SELECT statement to surface the properties of the complex JSON that we have, such as metadata or the Point property.

Try adding additional queries to your data source to enable querying of complex JSON types.

Now that we have created an Azure Search service that indexes our DocumentDB collection(s), we can build a nice **query-as-you-type** field on our portal. Try this yourself.

Enhancing security

As we have seen throughout this book, access to DocumentDB is provided by supplying a URI and a key. Microsoft Azure offers the capability to move your secrets away from your application and into Azure Key Vault. Azure Key Vault helps to protect cryptographic keys, secrets, and other information you want to store in a safe place outside your application boundaries (connection strings are also good candidates). Key Vault can help us to protect the DocumentDB URI and its key.

> DocumentDB has no (in-place) encryption feature at the time of writing, although a lot of people have already asked for it to be on the roadmap.

Creating and configuring Key Vault

Before we can use Key Vault, we need to create and configure it first. The easiest way to achieve this is by using PowerShell cmdlets. Please visit `https://msdn.microsoft.com/en-us/mt173057.aspx` to read more about PowerShell.

The following PowerShell cmdlets demonstrate how to set up and configure a Key Vault:

Command	Description
`Get-AzureSubscription`	This command will prompt you to log in using your Microsoft account. It returns a list of all Azure subscriptions that are available to you.
`Select-AzureSubscription -SubscriptionName "Windows Azure MSDN Premium"`	This tells PowerShell to use this subscription subject to our next steps.

`Switch-AzureMode AzureResourceManager`
 	
`New-AzureResourceGroup -Name 'IoTIncResourceGroup' -Location 'West Europe'`
	This creates a new Azure Resource Group with a name and a location.

`New-AzureKeyVault -VaultName 'IoTIncKeyVault' -ResourceGroupName 'IoTIncResourceGroup' -Location 'West Europe'`	This creates a new Key Vault inside the resource group and provides a name and location.

Command	Description
`$secretvalue = ConvertTo-SecureString '<DOCUMENTDB KEY>' -AsPlainText –Force`	This creates a security string for my DocumentDB key.
`$secret = Set-AzureKeyVaultSecret -VaultName 'IoTIncKeyVault' -Name 'DocumentDBKey' -SecretValue $secretvalue`	This creates a key named `DocumentDBKey` into the vault and assigns it the secret value we have just received.
`Set-AzureKeyVaultAccessPolicy -VaultName 'IoTIncKeyVault' -ServicePrincipalName <SPN> -PermissionsToKeys decrypt,sign`	This configures the application with the `Service Principal Name <SPN>` to get the appropriate rights to decrypt and sign
`Set-AzureKeyVaultAccessPolicy -VaultName 'IoTIncKeyVault' -ServicePrincipalName <SPN> -PermissionsToSecrets Get`	This configures the application with the SPN to also be able to get a key.

> Key Vault must be used together with Azure Active Directory to work. The SPN we need in the steps for PowerShell is actually a client ID of an application I have set up in my Azure Active Directory. Please visit https://azure.microsoft.com/nl-nl/documentation/articles/active-directory-integrating-applications/ to see how you can create an application.
>
> Make sure to copy the client ID (which is retrievable afterwards) and the key (which is *not* retrievable afterwards). We use these two pieces of information to take the next steps.

Using Key Vault from ASP.NET

In order to use the Key Vault we created in the previous section, we need to install some NuGet packages into our solution and/or projects:

```
Install-Package Microsoft.IdentityModel.Clients.ActiveDirectory -Version
2.16.204221202
```

```
Install-Package Microsoft.Azure.KeyVault
```

These two packages enable us to use AD and Key Vault from our ASP.NET application. The next step is to add some configuration information to our web.config file:

```
<add key="ClientId" value="<CLIENTID OF THE APP CREATED IN AD" />
    <add key="ClientSecret" value="<THE SECRET FROM AZURE AD PORTAL>"
/>

    <!-- SecretUri is the URI for the secret in Azure Key Vault -->
    <add key="SecretUri" value="https://iotinckeyvault.vault.azure.
net:443/secrets/DocumentDBKey" />
```

> If you deploy the ASP.NET application to Azure, you could even configure these settings from the Azure portal itself, completely removing it from the web.config file. This technique adds an additional ring of security around your application.

The following code snippet shows how to use AD and Key Vault inside the registration functionality of our scenario:

```
//no more keys in code or .config files. Just a appid, secret and the
unique URL to our key (SecretUri). When deploying to Azure we could
        //even skip this by setting appid and clientsecret in the
Azure Portal.
        var kv = new KeyVaultClient(new KeyVaultClient.
AuthenticationCallback(Utils.GetToken));
        var sec = kv.GetSecretAsync(WebConfigurationManager.
AppSettings["SecretUri"]).Result.Value;
```

The Utils.GetToken method is shown next. This method retrieves an access token from AD by supplying the ClientId and the secret. Since we configured Key Vault to allow this application to get the keys, the call to GetSecretAsync() will succeed. The code is as follows:

```
public async static Task<string> GetToken(string authority, string
resource, string scope)
        {
        var authContext = new AuthenticationContext(authority);
        ClientCredential clientCred = new ClientCredential(WebConf
igurationManager.AppSettings["ClientId"],
                    WebConfigurationManager.
AppSettings["ClientSecret"]);
```

```
            AuthenticationResult result = await authContext.
    AcquireTokenAsync(resource, clientCred);

            if (result == null)
                throw new InvalidOperationException("Failed to obtain
    the JWT token");

            return result.AccessToken;
        }
```

Instead of storing the key to DocumentDB somewhere in code or in the `web.config` file, it is now moved away to Key Vault. We could do the same with the URI to our DocumentDB and with other sensitive information as well (for example, storage account keys or connection strings).

Encrypting sensitive data

The documents we created in the previous section contains sensitive data like namespaces, Event Hub names, and tokens.

We could also use Key Vault to encrypt these specific values to enhance our security. In case someone gets hold of a document containing the device information, they would still be unable to mimic this device since the keys are encrypted.

> Try to use Key Vault to encrypt the sensitive information that is stored in DocumentDB before it is saved in there.

Migrating data

This section discusses how to use a tool to migrate data from an existing data source to DocumentDB. For this scenario, we assume that we already have a large datastore containing existing devices and their registration information (Event Hub connection information). In this section, we will see how to migrate an existing data store to our new DocumentDB environment. We use the DocumentDB Data Migration Tool for this.

You can download this tool from the Microsoft Download Center (http://www.microsoft.com/en-us/download/details.aspx?id=46436) or from GitHub if you want to check the code.

The tool is intuitive and enables us to migrate from several data sources:

- JSON files
- MongoDB
- SQL Server
- CSV files
- Azure Table storage
- Amazon DynamoDB
- HBase
- DocumentDB collections

To demonstrate its use, we migrate our existing Netherlands collection to our United Kingdom collection.

Start the tool and enter the right connection string to our DocumentDB database. We do this for both our source and target information in the tool. The connection strings you need to provide should look like this:

```
AccountEndpoint=https://<YOURDOCDBURL>;AccountKey=<ACCOUNTKEY>;Database=<NAMEOFDATABASE>.
```

You can click on the **Verify** button to make sure these are correct.

In the **Source Information** field, we provide Netherlands as being the source to pull data from. In the **Target Information** field, we specify United Kingdom as the target. In the following screenshot, you can see how these settings are provided in the migration tool for the source information:

The following screenshot shows the settings for the target information:

> It is also possible to migrate data to a collection that is not created yet. The migration tool can do this if you enter a collection name that is not available inside your database. You also need to select the pricing tier. Optionally, setting the partition key could help to distribute your documents based on this key across all collections you add in this screen.

This information is sufficient to run our example. Go to the **Summary** tab and verify the information you entered. Press **Import** to start the migration process.

We can verify a successful import on the **Import results** pane:

This example is a simple migration scenario but the tool is also capable of using complex queries to only migrate those documents that need to be moved or migrated.

> Try migrating data from an Azure Table storage table to DocumentDB by using this tool.

Summary

In this chapter, we saw how to integrate DocumentDB with other Microsoft Azure features. We discussed how to set up the Azure Search service and how create an index to our collection. We also covered how to use the Azure Search feature to enable full-text search on our documents, which could enable users to *query while typing*. Next, we saw how to add additional security to our scenario by using Key Vault. We also discussed how to create and configure Key Vault by using PowerShell cmdlets, and we saw how to enable our ASP.NET scenario application to make use of the Key Vault .NET SDK. Then, we discussed how to retrieve the sensitive information from Key Vault instead of the configuration files. Finally, we saw how to migrate an existing data source to our collection by using the DocumentDB Data Migration Tool.

Index

A

alerts
 account, monitoring 34-36
 creating 37, 38
 managing 34
application, DocumentDB
 account, provisioning 16, 17
 building 16
 collection, creating 18
 console application, building 19
 database, creating 18
ASP.NET
 Key Vault, using from 123, 124
**Atomicity, Consistency, Isolation,
  Durability (ACID) 6**
Azure Active Directory
 URL 123
Azure blade portal
 URL 14
Azure blogs
 URL 46
Azure portal
 URL 10
Azure Search
 setting up 116-121
 URL 117
Azure Table storage
 defining 11

B

bounded staleness consistency
 using 107
built-in functions
 using 56

C

consistency levels
 BOUNDED 33
 bounded staleness consistency, using 107
 EVENTUAL 33
 eventual staleness consistency, using 108
 SESSION 33
 session consistency, using 108
 setting 106, 107
 STRONG 33
 strong consistency, using 107
consistent indexing mode 89
console application
 building 19
 document, saving 20-23
 solution, setting up 19, 20
constraints, REST
 cacheable 65
 client-server 64
 stateless 64
 uniform interface 65

D

databases
 creating 9, 10
 obtaining 69
 permissions, setting 10
 users, administering 10
data migration
 defining 125-127
data model
 collections, managing 11
 databases, creating 9, 10

index update mode
  configuring 89
  consistent indexing mode 89
  Lazy indexing mode 90
  None indexing mode 90, 91
Internet of Things (IoT)
  about 7
  defining 109
  IoT Inc. 109, 110
  technical requirements 111
  URL 7
  Web API, building 114

J

JavaScript
  Stored procedures (SP) 3
  triggers 3
  User-defined functions (UDF) 3

K

keys
  managing 25
  read-only keys, managing 27
  recycling 26
Key Vault
  configuring 122, 123
  creating 122, 123
  used, from ASP.NET 123, 124

L

LINQ
  using 42
  using, to DocumentDB 61
  using, to object 41
loop 73

M

Microsoft Azure account
  URL 16
MongoDB
  defining 11

N

Node.js
  about 73
  defining 73, 74
  DocumentDB, utilizing from 77
  project, preparing 78
  URL 73
  using 74
Node.js application
  building 74
  first app, creating 75
  web app, creating 75-77
Node Package Manager (NPM) 74
NoSQL database
  characteristics 2

P

performance, DocumentDB
  managing 102-104
PersonInformation
  updating 42
PowerShell cmdlets
  defining 122
  URL 122
price model, DocumentDB
  account charges 13
  defining 13
  number of collections 13, 14
  resources, expanding 14, 15
  storage, defining 14
properties, performance
  CollectionSizeUsage 103
  CollectionUsage 103
  CurrentResourceQuotaUsage 103
  IndexTransformationProgress 103
  RequestCharge 103

R

Representational State Transfer. *See* **REST**
request headers
  Authorization 67
  Content-Type 67
  URL 67

[PACKT] PUBLISHING enterprise ✖
professional expertise distilled

Thank you for buying
Learning Azure DocumentDB

About Packt Publishing

Packt, pronounced 'packed', published its first book, *Mastering phpMyAdmin for Effective MySQL Management*, in April 2004, and subsequently continued to specialize in publishing highly focused books on specific technologies and solutions.

Our books and publications share the experiences of your fellow IT professionals in adapting and customizing today's systems, applications, and frameworks. Our solution-based books give you the knowledge and power to customize the software and technologies you're using to get the job done. Packt books are more specific and less general than the IT books you have seen in the past. Our unique business model allows us to bring you more focused information, giving you more of what you need to know, and less of what you don't.

Packt is a modern yet unique publishing company that focuses on producing quality, cutting-edge books for communities of developers, administrators, and newbies alike. For more information, please visit our website at www.packtpub.com.

About Packt Enterprise

In 2010, Packt launched two new brands, Packt Enterprise and Packt Open Source, in order to continue its focus on specialization. This book is part of the Packt Enterprise brand, home to books published on enterprise software – software created by major vendors, including (but not limited to) IBM, Microsoft, and Oracle, often for use in other corporations. Its titles will offer information relevant to a range of users of this software, including administrators, developers, architects, and end users.

Writing for Packt

We welcome all inquiries from people who are interested in authoring. Book proposals should be sent to author@packtpub.com. If your book idea is still at an early stage and you would like to discuss it first before writing a formal book proposal, then please contact us; one of our commissioning editors will get in touch with you.

We're not just looking for published authors; if you have strong technical skills but no writing experience, our experienced editors can help you develop a writing career, or simply get some additional reward for your expertise.

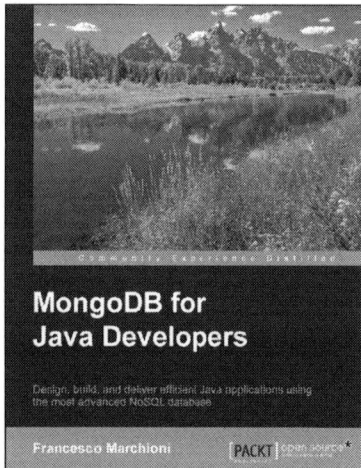

MongoDB for Java Developers

ISBN: 978-1-78528-027-6   Paperback: 192 pages

Design, build, and deliver efficient Java applications using the most advanced NoSQL database

1. Reuse the skills you have acquired through Hibernate or Spring to promote your applications to use NoSQL storage.

2. Explore the list of libraries that are already available to assist you in developing Java EE applications with MongoDB.

3. A step-by-step tutorial to create leaner and faster applications using MongoDB.

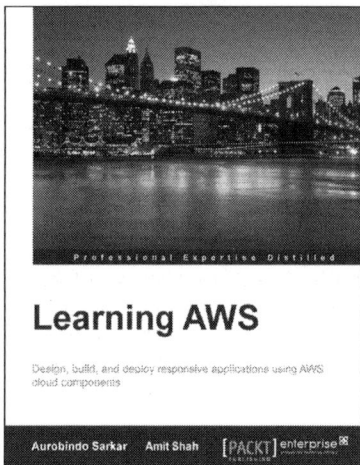

Learning AWS

ISBN: 978-1-78439-463-9   Paperback: 236 pages

Design, build, and deploy responsive applications using AWS cloud components

1. Build scalable and highly available real-time applications.

2. Make cost-effective architectural decisions by implementing your product's functional and non-functional requirements.

3. Develop your skills with hands-on exercises using a three-tiered service oriented application as an example.

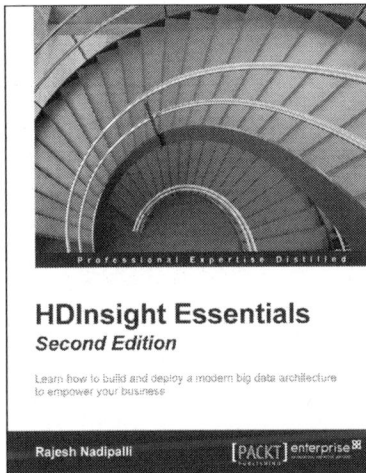

HDInsight Essentials
Second Edition
ISBN: 978-1-78439-942-9   Paperback: 178 pages

Learn how to build and deploy a modern big data architecture to empower your business

1. Learn how to quickly provision a Hadoop cluster using Windows Azure Cloud Services.

2. Build an end-to-end application for a big data problem using open source software.

3. Discover more about modern data architecture with this guide, to help you understand the transition from legacy relational Enterprise Data Warehouse.

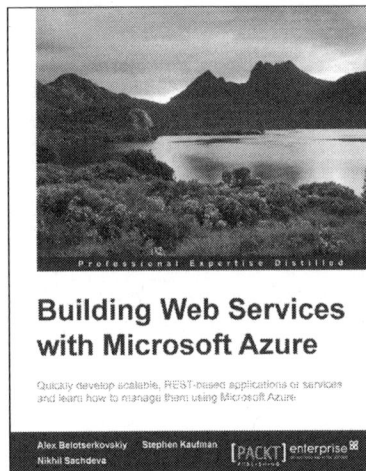

Building Web Services with Microsoft Azure
ISBN: 978-1-78439-837-8   Paperback: 322 pages

Quickly develop scalable, REST-based applications or services and learn how to manage them using Microsoft Azure

1. Explore the tools to rapidly build, deploy, and manage cloud solutions using Microsoft Azure.

2. Learn how to utilize Entity Framework, SQL Azure database, and other storage mechanisms to build out the data tier of your solution.

3. A step-by-step guide focused on delivering solutions to your cloud development lifecycle with the best practices for web services and APIs.

Please check **www.PacktPub.com** for information on our titles

Made in the USA
San Bernardino, CA
26 January 2016